Contents

1 An introduction to business models

A business model is a sustainable way of doing business. Here sustainability stresses the ambition to survive over time and create a successful, perhaps even profitable, entity in the long run. The reason for this apparent ambiguity around the concept of profitability is, of course, that business models apply to many different settings than the profit-oriented company. The application of business models is much broader and is a meaningful concept both in relation to public-sector administration, NGO's, schools and universities and us, as individuals. A recent contribution in this latter realm is the book Business Model You by Clark *et al.* (2012), which translates the ideas of Osterwalder & Pigneur's (2010) business model canvas into a personal setting for career enhancement purposes.

Whether, in the case of the privately owned company, profits are retained by the shareholders or distributed in some degree to a broader mass of stakeholders is not the focus here. Rather, it is the point of this book to illustrate how one may go about conceptualizing, analyzing or communicating the business model of a company, organisation, or person!

Sustainability is here interpreted as the propensity to survive and thus also the ability to stay competitive. As such, a business model cannot be a static way of doing business. It must be developed, nursed and optimized continuously in order for the company to meet changing competitive demands. Precisely how the company differentiates itself is the competitive strategy, whilst it is the business model that defines on which basis this is to be achieved; i.e. how it combines its know-how and resources to deliver the value proposition (which will secure profits and thus make the company sustainable).

In the last decades, the speed of change in the business landscape has continuously accelerated. In the late 1990's, the e-business revolution changed global competition, and during the early years of the new millennium the knowledge-based society along with rising globalization and the developments in the BRIC economies ensured that momentum continued upwards. As new forms of value configurations emerge, so do new business models. Therefore, new analysis models that identify corporate resources such as knowledge and core processes are needed in order to illustrate the effects of decisions on value creation. Accordingly, managers as well as analysts must recognize that business models are made up of portfolios of different resources and assets and, not merely traditional physical and financial assets, and every company needs to create their own specific business model that links its unique combination of assets and activities to value creation.

The rising interest in understanding and evaluating business models can to some extent be traced to the fact that new value configurations outcompete existing ways of doing business. There exist cases where some businesses are more profitable than others in the same industry, even though they apply the same strategy. This illustrates that a business model is different from a competitive strategy and a value chain. A value chain is a set of serially performed activities for a firm in a specific industry.

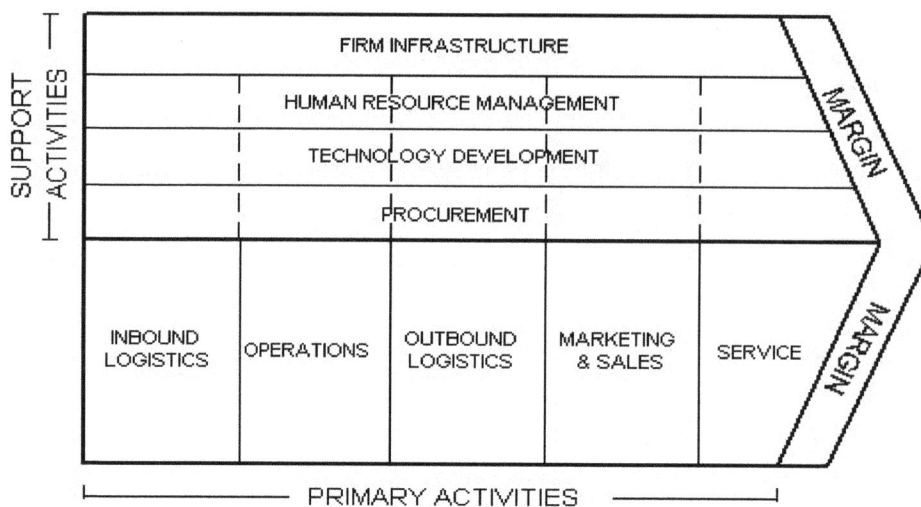

The Generic Value Chain

Figure 1: Porters Generic Value Chain, Porter 1988

The difference thus lies in the way activities are performed (strategic and tactical choices), and therefore a business model is closely connected to a management control agenda. The business model perspective has also been found useful for aligning financial and non-financial performance measures with strategy and goals. In addition, communicative aspects from executive management to the rest of the organization, and also to external stakeholders such as bankers, investors, and analysts, are also facilitated by a business model perspective.

1.1 Overview of the book

The field of business models is becoming a core management discipline alongside accounting, finance, organization etc. and we soon expect to see teaching modules on business models entering leading Masters and MBA programmes. This development is taking place as we speak, and at Aalborg University, this curriculum is already a mandatory part of several Masters level courses. This movement is in the coming years expected to be driven forth, partly by a call for greater interdisciplinarity within the core management disciplines and across the natural sciences, and partly because business model optimization and commercialization will become a politically driven issue in the light of innovation and sustainability pressures. At CREBS we believe that the focus on Business Models in policy-making and the business environment should be equally as important as the present focus on innovation and technology development and will become a focal point of support for entrepreneurs and small and medium sized companies.

The "Vision" of this book is to be the most accessed and read book on business models by students, teachers and practitioners, and in due course to strengthen the relationship between innovation and commercialization activities and to make an impact on growth and sustainability of businesses.

The "Mission" of this book is to constitute an internationally renowned platform that accompanies leading experts world wide and to affect business-related policy-making on regional, national and transnational levels.

This book is structured so that the first 4 chapters give a basic introduction to the field of business models. Then we illustrate how the three main tendencies in business – networking, innovation and globalizing – are achieved through a business model perspective. Finally, we explore the inks between business models and profitability to greater extent.

1.2   Networking, innovating and globalizing

Organizational survival has been stressed several times in the introduction to this book. Why? Because it is adamant. Of course, some companies and organizations are situated in sweet spots, with lacking competition, lots of funding and market growth in terms of customers to serve. This is, incidentally, regardless of whether the organization is in the public sector or the private sector. However, the situation is more often than not one of competition, constant change in markets and demand and fights for resources, competences and capital. Especially in the western world this is inherent.

Whoever thought that the financial crisis, which started back in 2007, was over has during the second half of 2011 been proven wrong. National banks, governments and corporations world-wide have continuously smaller room for maneuver and weaker tools for creating financial stability and growth as the crisis moves into new phases. As such, more citizens will in 2012 be questioning not just the future of the financial sector of the western world, but also the sustainability of the industrialized western society as a whole. On the one hand, pressure from under-burdened western society taxpayers (voters) who crave an average working week of 35-37 hours and retirement 40-50 years prior to their death will be on the rise.

On the other hand, eager hardworking Asian and Indian consumers with surprisingly well-educated workforces will lead us to be questioning our chances of economic survival in a truly globalized world all throughout 2012. One possible answer to this problem is that we to a greater extent need to rely on human capital in the quest for private sector value creation and competitiveness. However, human capital will not make the difference alone. Only when complemented by triple-helix based innovation structures, creativity and unique business models that commercialize innovation and human capital will this be an avenue to future sustainability of these societies.

So you see: business models are not only important; they are crucial! Henry Chesbrough, Professor at University of California, Berkeley, has at several occasions stated that he would rather have part in a mediocre invention with a great business model, than a great invention with a mediocre business model. It is in this light that the keywords networking, innovation and globalizing are brought forth. These are the key success factors for sustaining business growth moving forward and hence also society as we know it.

The title of this book specifically emphasizes the three aspects networking, innovating and globalizing. We view these aspects as key success factors for sustaining business growth and thus they become cornerstones of the successful business models of the future. Networking and the ability to collaborate with key strategic partners in win-win based relationships will become even more vital for companies in the next years and decades. Building and encompassing e.g. win-win based relationships with strategic partners will require dedicated business model innovation and these aspects will be under severe pressure from the rising degree of globalization we are seeing in these years.

In the end the three success factors for sustaining business growth together have the potential to produce a whole new array of business model archetypes. The world has already seen the birth of the so-called *Born Globals* (REF here) and we expect to see other archetypes like *Growth-symbioses* and *Micro-multinationals*[1] emerge in the near future.

1.3   Value configuration

New value configurations such as those born out of the three success factors for future growth highlighted above reflect changes in the competitive landscape towards more variety in value creation models within industries. Previously the name of the industry may have served as a recipe for addressing customers. It doesn't any more. Already in 2000, leading management thinker, Gary Hamel, quoted that competition now increasingly stands between competing business concepts. If firms within the same industry operate on the basis of different business models, different competences and knowledge resources are key parts of the value creation, and thus comparison of the specific firms even within peer groups now requires interpretation based on an understanding of differences in business models.

If firms only disclose accounting numbers and key performance indicators without disclosing the business model that explains the interconnectedness of the indicators and why the bundle of activities performed is relevant for understanding the strategy for value creation of the firm, this interpretation must be done by someone else. Currently, there does not exist much research based insight into how this reading and interpretation may be conducted, and it is very likely that this understanding of the value creation of firms would be facilitated if companies disclosed such information as an integral part of their strategy disclosure. We attempt to address these issues in detail in chapter 9.

---

1   At Center for Research Excellence in Business modelS we are currently working on series of research projects that map out the attributes of the two new business model archetypes Growth-symbioses and Micro-multinationals.

1.3.1 (One possible) verbal definition of a business model

A business model describes the coherence in the strategic choices which facilitates the handling of the processes and relations which create value on both the operational, tactical and strategic levels in the organization. The business model is therefore the platform which connects resources, processes and the supply of a service which results in the fact that the company is profitable in the long term.

This definition emphasizes the need to focus on understanding the connections and the interrelations of the bsuienss and its operations so that the core of a business model description is the connections that create value. This can be thought of e.g. by contemplating the silos by which the management discussion in the annual report normally is structured. By themselves, endless descriptions of customer relations, employee competences, knowledge sharing, innovation activities and corporate risks do not tell the story of the business model. However, if we start asking how these different elements interrelate, which changes among them that are important to keep an eye on and what is the status on operations, strategy and the activities initiated in order to conquer a unique value proposition are effectuated, we will start to get a feeling for how the chosen business model is performing.

1.3.2 Conceptualizing the business model

Conceptualizing the business model is therefore concerned with identifying this platform, while analyzing it is concerned with gaining an understanding of precisely which levers of control are apt to deliver the value proposition of the company. Finally, communicating the business model is concerned with identifying the most important performance measures, both absolute and relative measures, and relating them to the overall value creation story.

A business model is neither just a value chain, nor is it a corporate strategy. There exist many value configurations that are different to that of a value chain, like e.g. value networks and hubs. Rather, a business model is concerned with the unique combination of attributes that deliver a certain value proposition. Therefore, a business model is the platform which enables the strategic choices to become profitable.

In some instances it can be difficult to distinguish between businesses that succeed because they are the best at executing a generic strategy and businesses that succeed because they have unique business models. This is an important distinction to make, and while some cases are clear-cut, others remain fuzzier.

One of the best examples of a business model that has changed an existing industry is Ryanair, which has essentially restructured the business model of the airline industry. As the air transport markets have matured, incumbent companies that have developed sophisticated and complex business models now face tremendous pressure to find less costly approaches that meet broad customer needs with minimal complexity in products and processes. While the generic strategy of Ryanair can be denoted as a low-price strategy, this does not render much insight into the business model of the company.

The low-cost option is per se open to all existing airlines, and many already compete alongside Ryanair on price. However, Ryanair was among the first airline companies to mold its business platform to create a sustainable low-price business. Many unique business models are easy to communicate because they have a unique quality about them; i.e. either a unique concept or value proposition. This is also the case for Ryanair. It is the "no-service business model". In fact, the business model is so well thought through that even the arrogance and attitude of the top management matches the rest of the business. But they can make money in an industry that has been under pressure for almost a decade, and for this they deserve recognition. Ryanair's business model narrative is the story of a novel flying experience – irrespective of the attitude of the customer after the ordeal.

A much applied example in the management literature is Toyota. However, Toyota did not really change the value proposition of the car industry. They were able to achieve superior quality through JIT and Lean management technologies, and they may have made slightly smaller cars than the American car producers, but their value proposition and operating platform were otherwise unchanged. The same can be said for Ford in the early 20th century. Ford's business setup was not really a new business model. It sold one car model in one color, but so did most other car manufacturers at the time. Ford was able to reduce costs through a unique organization of the production setup, but the value proposition was not unique.

In the 1990's, Dell changed the personal computer industry by applying the Internet as a novel distribution channel. This platform as a foundation of the pricing strategy took out several parts of the sales channel, leaving a larger cut to Dell and cheaper personal computers to the customers. Nowadays this distribution strategy is not a unique business model anymore as many other laptop producers apply it. Therefore, it is also a good example of the fact that what is unique today is not necessarily unique tomorrow.

This mirrors Christensen's quote that "today's competitive advantage becomes tomorrow's albatross" (Christensen 2001, 105). Having the right business model at the present does not necessarily guarantee success for years on end as new technology or changes in the business environment and customer base can influence profitability. The point to be made here is that if the value proposition is not affected in some manner, then it is most likely not a new business model. However, it could be the case that the value proposition is not affected, but the business' value generating attributes are radically different from those of the competitors. Three examples of this are:

1. The value proposition of two companies producing kitchen appliances. One may be more high-end than the other, but this is a part of the competitive strategy, not the actual business model
2. The value proposition of two companies producing laptops. One may be priced lower because the range is smaller and the design kept to one color etc. This is not equivalent to different business models, but also a question of competitive strategy and customer selection. However, if one of the producers decides to alter the traditional distribution model, cutting out store placement and setting up technical support as local franchisees only, that could be a new business model
3. Two hair salons will both be performing haircuts, but their value propositions may be vastly different according to the physical setup around the core attribute

1.3.3 Which parameters do we need to understand?

Remembering that the business model is the platform which enables the strategic choices to become profitable, then it is clear that a business model is neither a pricing strategy, a new distribution channel, an information technology, nor is it a quality control scheme in the production setup. By themselves that is. A business model is concerned with the value proposition of the company, but it is not the value proposition alone as it in itself is supported by a number of parameters and characteristics, e.g. some of the parameters mentioned above like applied distribution channels, customer relationships, pricing models and sourcing from strategic partnerships. The key question here is therefore: how is the strategy and value proposition of the company leveraged?

The problem with trying to visualize the "business model" of the company is that it can very quickly become a generic and static organization diagram illustrating the process of transforming inputs to outputs in a chain-like fashion. The reader is thus more often than not left wondering how the organization actually functions. Hence, the core of the business model description should be the connections between the different elements that the management review is traditionally divided into, i.e. the actual activities being performed in the company. Companies often report a lot of information about activities such as customer relations, distribution channels, employee competencies, knowledge sharing, innovation and risks; but this information may seem unimportant if the company fails to show how the various elements of the value creation collaborate, and which changes we should keep an eye on. One such idea on how to visualize the business model is the popular Business Model Canvas by Osterwalder & Pigneur (2010).

When we perceive relationships and linkages, they often reflect some kind of tangible transactions, i.e. the flow of products, services or money. When perceiving and analyzing the value transactions going on inside an organization, or between an organization and its partners, there is a marked tendency to neglect or forget the often parallel intangible transactions and interrelations that are also involved.

At the Center for Research Excellence in Business modelS (CREBS) we have recently analyzed how existing "models" or "tools" perceive transactions and relationships, and we have found that they generally lack a conception of intangible transactions, which in many cases are the very key to understanding the value logic of a business model. These ideas are discussed in depth in chapter 6 on value creation maps.

While value creation from an accounting perspective merely constitutes the realization of value at the time of sale of the product, i.e. registration of turnover, from a process perspective, value creation may be characterized as the steps leading towards value realization. Thereby we are in this genre more concerned with value creation potential, value creation processes and value creation extraction, which all can be said to precede the value realization phase.

In 2002 Chesbrough & Rosenbloom tried to corner the important aspects to be considered in order to comprehensively describe the business model of the company. They defined the business model as "[a] construct that integrates these earlier perspectives into a coherent framework that takes technological characteristics and potentials as inputs, and converts them through customers and markets into economic outputs. The business model is thus conceived as a focusing device that mediates between technology development and economic value creation. We argue that firms need to understand the cognitive role of the business model, in order to commercialize technology in ways that will allow firms to capture value from their technology investments" (Chesbrough & Rosenbloom 2002, 5). This definition is worth noticing because it was among the first one to set value creation as a central notion of understanding the points of concern in the business model of a company.

In the wake of this definition, they define six elements which make up the business model:

1. Articulate the value proposition, that is, the value created for users by the offering based on the technology
2. Identify a market segment, that is, the users to whom the technology is useful and for what purpose
3. Define the structure of the value chain within the firm required to create and distribute the offering
4. Estimate the cost structure and profit potential of producing the offering, given the value proposition and value chain structure chosen
5. Describe the position of the firm within the value network linking suppliers and customers, including identification of potential complementors and competitors
6. Formulate the competitive strategy by which the innovating firm will gain and hold advantage over rivals

It is interesting to note that Chesbrough & Rosenbloom in the above take in strategy as an element of the business model. The relationship between business models and strategy is, if not fuzzy, then at least undecided. In her book from 2002, Joan Magretta defines business models as "stories that explain how enterprises work", and notes that strategy, understood as how to outmaneuver your competitors, is something different from a business model. Seddon *et al.* 2004 take part in this discussion by schematizing the possibilities in figure 3 below.

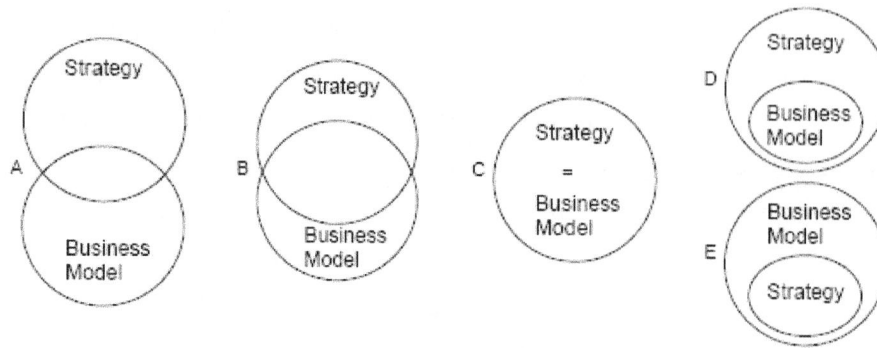

Figure 3: Possible concept overlaps between business models and strategy (Seddon *et al.* 2004)

If we briefly recap the business model definition given above: "A business model describes the coherence in the strategic choices which facilitates the handling of the processes and relations which create value on both the operational, tactical and strategic levels in the organization. The business model is therefore the platform which connects resources, processes and the supply of a service which results in the fact that the company is profitable in the long term", it is evident that it takes the stance of Seddon *et al.*s (2004) option E, because it sees the business model as the platform that enables strategy-execution.

1.4   Driving out the business model

In order to start working with clarifying the business model of a company or an organization, one can start off by asking the following questions (regardless of which business model framework one chooses for structuring and visualizing the business model during the process):

- Which value creation proposition are we trying to sell to our customers and the users of our products?
- Which connections are we trying to optimize through the value creation of the company?
- In which way is the product/service of the company unique in comparison to those of major competitors?
- Are there any critical connections between the different phases of value creation undertaken?
- Can we describe the activities that we set in motion in order to become better at what we do?
- ...and can we enlighten these through relevant performance measures?
- Which resources, systems and competences must we attain in order to be able to mobilize our strategy?
- What do we do in relation to ensuring access to and developing the necessary competences?
- Can we measure the effects of our striving to become better, more innovative or more efficient, apart from the bottom line?
- Which risks can undermine the success of the chosen Business Model?
- What can we do to control and minimize these?

1.5   Archetypes of business models: looking for patterns

Other authors have attempted to define business models by discussing and identifying overall business model generics and archetypes. Business model archetypes was, as will be described in greater detail in chapter 2 on the history of the business model concept, one of the primary discussions in the field in relation to e-business models.

Already in 1998, Timmers classified 10 generic types of Internet business models:

- e-shop
- e-procurement
- e-auction
- 3rd party marketplace
- e-mall
- Virtual communities
- Value chain integrator
- Information brokers
- Value chain service provider

- Collaboration platforms

Two years later, Rappa (2000) identified 41 types of Internet business models and classified them into 9 categories, which were fairly similar to Weill & Vitale's eight (e-)business models from 2001:

- Content Provider
- Direct to Consumer
- Full Service Provider
- Intermediary
- Shared Infrastructure
- Value net integrator
- Virtual Community
- Whole of Enterprise/Government

In recent years it is to a rising degree being realized that archetypes of e-business in reality merely are translations of already existing business models. And thus business model archetypes seen through today's lenses could be something along the lines of:

- Buyer-seller models
- Advanced buyer-seller models
- Network-based business models
- Multisided business models
- Business models based on ecology
- Bottom of the pyramid business models
- Business Models based on social communities
- Co-creation and consumer-collaboration models
- Freemium models

Osterwalder *et al.* 2010 and Johnson 2010 provide more inputs on business model archetypes or patterns as they may also be called.

Sum-up questions for chapter 1

- What is the difference between strategy and business models?
- What is the difference between a business model and a value chain?
- What is a business model archetype?
- Find real life examples of the various business model archetypes

2 A brief history of the business model concept

Business models have been intimately connected with e-business since the rise of the Internet during the late 1990's. Kodama (1999) and Hedman & Kalling 2003 provide early reviews of the business model concept as seen around the dot.com era and the rise of the e-business model, while a more recent account of events and developments can be found in Fielt's 2011 review.

Around 2001-2002, the concept of the business model started receiving a much more general meaning in management literature than the e-biz rhetoric which had surrounded it in the first years. Despite the definition of a business model still being "fuzzy at best", in the words of Porter (2001), his colleague Joan Magretta, for instance, gained much attention by perceiving business models as "stories that explain how enterprises work" (Magretta 2002, 4). According to Magretta, business models did not only show how the firm made money but also answered fundamental questions such as: "who is the customer? and "what does the customer value?" (Magretta 2002, 4). Precisely this aspect of value seen from the point of the customer made a big impact on the existing thinking.

Further, a basic idea of the business model concept was that it should spell out the unique value proposition of the firm and how such a value proposition ought to be implemented. For customers such "value creation" could be related to solving a problem, improving performance, or reducing risk and costs, which might require specific value configurations including relationships to suppliers, access to technologies, insight in the users' needs etc.

In the late 1990's the 'business model' concept became almost synonymous with e-business and the emergence of the so-called new economy. The Internet had in essence created an array of new business models where the major focal point of the literature on business models from an e-business perspective became how to migrate successfully to profitable e-business models. Therefore, much of the business model literature focusing on the e-business context concerned how such organizations could create value in comparison to their bricks and mortar counterparts. The only problem with the early e-business models was that they tended to forget the actual profit-formula or at best be completely overoptimistic on the conversion of Internet traffic to actual profits.

As such, far from all ways of doing business through the Internet were profitable, and accordingly there has been a substantial interest in explaining how the nature of the new distribution and communication channels formed parts of new business structures. One way of approaching this issue was through Amit & Zott's (2001) four dimensions of value-creation potential in e-businesses that has to be in place for an e-business model to be profitable: It must create efficiencies in comparison to existing ways of doing business, and it must facilitate complementarities, novelty or enable the lock-in of customers. For example, the creation of efficiencies can be seen as the underlying notion of Internet-based business models in the banking industry, while e-commerce as a new distribution channel has created efficiencies thus enabling new business models to emerge.

In the late 1990's the mere naming of companies as 'dot-com' was enough to signal that the business model of the company was potentially profitable or at least attractive for investors. However, after the tech stock crash, analyst and investor behaviour changed so radically that signaling dot.com had the opposite effect. In a blow, it was no longer viable just to imitate an Internet-company business model. Now profit generation is required regardless of ones distribution channel. This led to several authors stating that the profit-formula should still be a central feature of the business model. Based on dominant revenue models on the Internet, Afuah and Tucci (2003) identified four profit-formulas for e-businesses:

- Commission
- Advertising
- Mark-up
- Production

It is worth noting that "[m]uch of what is being said about the New Economy is not that new at all. Waves of discontinuous change have occurred before", as Senge & Carstedt (2001, 24) state. Just think of how Henry Ford's business model revolutionized the car industry almost a century ago, or how Sam Walton revolutionized the retail industry in the 1960's with his information technology focus and choice of demographic attributes for store locations, thus creating an immense cost structure focus along with a monopolistic market situation. These notions are what Hal Varian denotes as discontinuous innovation.

Although the present focus on business models within academic and practitioner circles to a great extent can be related to their earlier discussions within an e-business context, the importance of the business model perspective is far from only relevant in certain distribution channel structures. The transformation of the inter- and intra-company value chain is ongoing in almost all areas of the economy and this considerably challenges the markets and its enterprises. "Much talk [of business models: Ed.] revolves around how traditional business models are being changed and the future of e-based business models" (Alt & Zimmermann 2001, 1) but this is merely half the story. Business models are perhaps the most discussed and least understood of the newer business concepts.

Taking one's point of departure in a business model perspective can have multiple purposes. Among the advantages of this approach is the possibility of enabling company management to structure their thoughts and understanding about strategic objectives and other relevant issues. Furthermore, this facilitates the conveyance of ideas and expectations the management has to the employees on the business process level and to the technically oriented functions. There are clear linkages to creating an understanding of the overall functioning of the firm in and, in addition, a focus on communicating the management perceptions of the business internally in the firm. Accentuating these thoughts on creating a common understanding of the business, its strategy and objectives within the entire enterprise, Hoerl (1999) further argues that the application of the business model helps to structure the addressing of key business issues and that an effective business model ought to incorporate aspects such as culture, values, and governance.

Conceptualizing the Business Model is therefore concerned with understanding the 'whole' of the business and its value creation logic. There exist a number of different value configuration types other than the value chain, and newer types of value configurations to a large extent reflect changes in the competitive landscape. There is a tendency that today a greater variety exists in value creation models within industries where previously the "name of the industry served as shortcut for the prevailing business model's approach to market structure" (Sandberg 2002, 3). Competition now increasingly stands between competing business concepts, as Gary Hamel (2000) argues in his book 'Leading the Revolution', and not only between constellations of firms linked together in linear value chains, as was the underlying notion in the original strategy framework by Porter (1985).

If firms within the same industry operate on the basis of different business models, different competences and knowledge resources are key parts of the value creation, and mere benchmarking of key performance indicators will not be able to provide any meaningful insight into the profit or growth potential of the firm. Comparisons of the specific firm with its peer group will more often than not require interpretation within an understanding of differences in business models.

It is by no means a new idea to create a model of the organization, which a business model, understood as a model of the business, may be perceived as. Organization charts and diagrams showing how departments and divisions interact with and affect each other are well known. However, a business model comprehends something more than just the diagram. It should at least include a coherent understanding of the strategy, structure and the ability to utilize technological solutions to create value, which are three very significant attributes. A prominent, almost state-of-the-art example illustrating precisely these three components, is Dell. Dell's strategy is direct sales, and the company is structured around the utilization of information technology, almost like a hub, in this way enabling online ordering, custom built pc's and direct shipping (Kraemer *et al.* 1999), i.e. an extension of the existing personal-computer business model via a unique strategy, structure and the application of information technology (Magretta 1998).

Unlike traditional organizational diagrams and charts that merely illustrate the actions of an organization and the formal organization, organigraphs enable the drawing of organizational action by demonstrating "how a place works, depicting critical interactions among people, products, and information" (Mintzberg & Van der Heyden 1999, 88). Organigraphs consist of four basic components: the set, the chain, the hub, and the web that are applied in visualizations of the organization in order to illustrate its concrete relationships and processes. The first two components are rather conventional and are also found in the more traditional organizational illustrations, while the two latter components are novel introductions.

The Four Philosophies of Managing

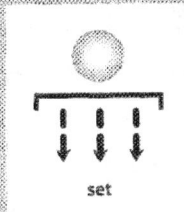

set

In the set, managers look it over – they allocate.

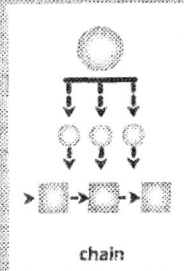

chain

In the chain, managers lay it on – they control.

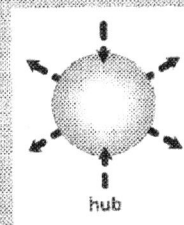

hub

In the hub, managers draw it in – they coordinate.

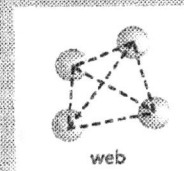

web

In the web, managers link it all – they energize.

Figure 4: Organigraphs (Mintzberg & Van der Heyden 1999)

The set refers to a collection of separate parts, a portfolio so to speak. For instance, this could be a set of independent activities, e.g. performed in two independent divisions or by two individual lawyers in the same company. As opposed to the set, the three remaining components are all characterized by some sort of connectivity. The first one, the chain, describes a sequential connectivity of activities, e.g. like in Ford's automobile factory. Applying chains as connections promotes standardization and enhances reliability. The third component, the hub, serves as a coordination center. This could be both in a physical form (e.g. a manager) and in the form of a conceptual point of reference (e.g. an intranet). Basically, "[h]ubs depict movement to and from one focal point. But often connections are more complicated than that" (Mintzberg & Van der Heyden 1999, 89). This is where the final component, the web, comes in. Examples of such a type of organizational connection are teams or the notion of interactive networks. This way of illustrating how organizations work has been applied by Thrane *et al.* (2002) to identify relevant performance measures, since managerial action must be determined by the dilemmas of control management faces.

According to Chesbrough & Rosenbloom (2002, 530), the origins of the business model concept can be traced back to Chandler's seminal book 'Strategy and Structure' from 1962. Strategy, Chandler states, "can be defined as the determination of the basic long-term goals and objectives of an enterprise, and the adoption of courses of action and the allocation of resources necessary for carrying out these goals" (Chandler 1962, 13). Further developments in the concept travel through Ansoff's (1965) thoughts on corporate strategy to Andrews' (1980) definitions of corporate and business strategy, which, according to Chesbrough & Rosenbloom (2002) can be seen as a predecessor of and equivocated to that of a business model definition.

Child's (1972) paper on organizational structure, environment and performance, incidentally to a great extent influenced by Chandler's work, is, however, among the earliest to gather and present these thoughts diagrammatically. Although he does not explicitly refer to his schematization of "the role of strategic choice in a theory of organization" (Child 1972, 18) as a business model representation, the thoughts presented here incorporate many of the central elements presented within the recent literature on this emerging concept. For instance, Child's term 'prior ideology' covers the aspects of vision and value proposition, objectives, and strategy of an organization, while 'operating effectiveness' is viewed as an outcome of the organizational strategy and the elements: scale of operations, technology, structure, and human resources.

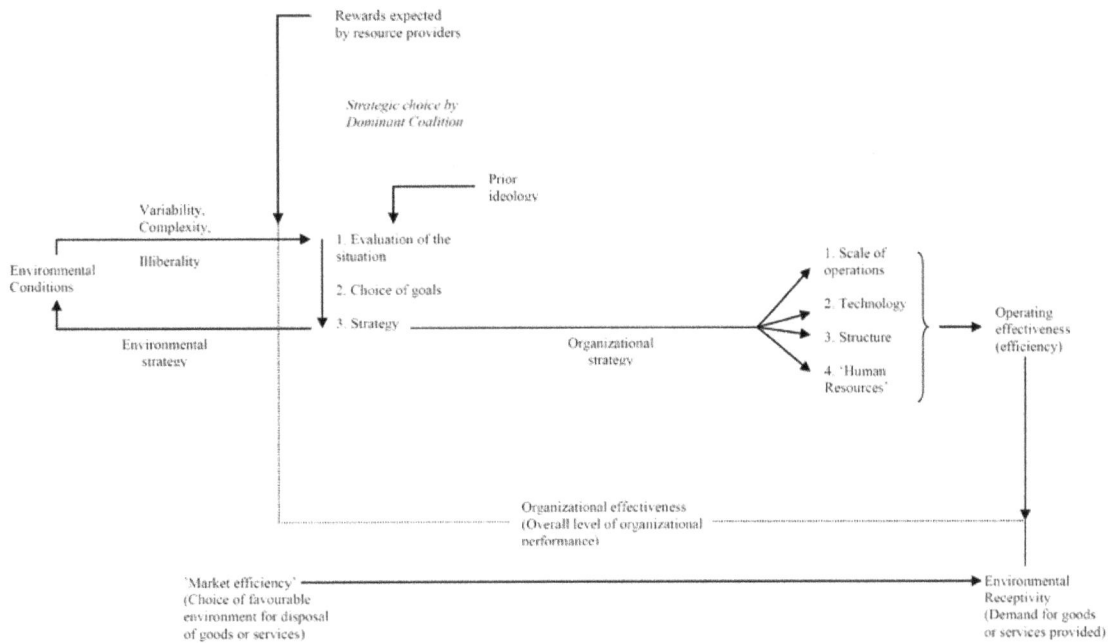

Figure 5: The Role of Strategic Choice in a Theory of Organization (Child 1972)

The role of technology in relation to the business model is not to be underestimated, as it is a key element in determining which organizational structures become feasible, because it influences the design of the business, i.e. its underlying architecture. Thompson's 'Organizations in Action' (1967) can in this respect be regarded as laying the foundation for studying the impact of technology on the feasibility of business model concepts. Thompson (1967) proposed a typology of different kinds of organizational technologies, distinguishing between long-linked, intensive and mediating technologies. These different technology types play different roles in connection with value creation and thus also the business model.

The management of fundamental strategic value configuration logics such as relationships to suppliers, access to technologies, insight into the users' needs etc., can be just as important and relevant as inventing new revolutionary business models.

Besides this brief review of the background of the business model movement, it is important to note that there exist multitudes of different angles within which the business model concept could be addressed. In Hedman & Kalling's (2003) review, the focus is on business models from an e-business and information technology perspective, while Osterwalder's 2003 review enhances the understanding of the business in order to improve information system design through a 'business model ontology'. However, an information system perspective merely reflects a minor segment of the business model movement as will be evident in particularly chapters 3 and 5 below, but also the chapter concerning business model innovation (chapter 6) and globalization of high-technology ventures (chapter 7).

The innovation perspective on business models, which encompasses both business development and new business ventures, is at the present one of the fields where the business model movement experiences the greatest momentum. However, this field of auditing was among the first fields to embrace the ideas of understanding business models and value creation. Also within the fields of voluntary reporting and disclosure and communication has the concept of business models been discussed and applied vividly.

Sum-up questions for chapter 2

- Why was the e-business revolution so important to the rise in focus on business models?
- Discuss the relation between strategy and structure from a business model perspective
- What is the difference between an organigraph and a business model?

3 Moving towards maturity in business model definitions

The field of business models has, as is the case with all emerging fields of practice, slowly matured through the development of frameworks, models, concepts and ideas over the last 15 years. New concepts, theories and models typically transcend a series of maturity phases. For the concept of Business Models, we are at the verge of moving from phase 2 to 3, after having spent a lot of time during the 1990's and 2000's arguing for the importance of understanding business models properly and discussing the content and potential building blocks of them. Therefore, in terms of maturity – the time for focusing on the more complex and dynamic aspects of business models seems to be right – right now!

Figure 6: The concept maturity line

In figure 6 above, the move from phase 2 to 3 significantly heightens the requirements for methodological coherence and structure and therefore it is also time to converge otherwise separate research streams and attempt to attain a common appreciation of business models. In the wake of this, a number of "business model associations" have emerged in recent years, e.g. around Osterwalder and Pigneur's Business Model

In an attempt to move the field into new ground 2011 saw the launching of the "Center for Research Excellence in Business modelS" (CREBS) as an interdisciplinary coordination hub for researchers and common research projects. CREBS' aim is to function as a natural hub between the technology-based research environments and the business oriented research environments, thereby conforming interests from different environments. CREBS is therefore a natural partner for coordinating interdisciplinary research projects.

CREBS is primarily a project-based research center with affiliates from numerous professional and geographical backgrounds and interests. This is seen as a key strength, and for CREBS to be able to undertake large scale research projects, it relies to a large extent on ad hoc affiliations leveraged from the existing network. In other words, CREBS leverages an asset-light business model for business model research!

This debate on attaining maturity is important for the field in the sense that this will be a prerequisite for it to become accepted as a discipline in line with accounting, innovation, entrepreneurship, finance etc. In the remainder of this chapter we first discuss business model definitions from the perspective of different typologies, here relating to the breadth and scope of the suggested frameworks. After this we discuss the characteristics of business models as seen in the early literature. By characteristics we do not mean building blocks *per se*, rather the idea is to discuss the roles and affiliations of the business model and how different contributions seek to place the business model in the context of other fields of practice.

3.1   Business model typologies

A substantial amount of literature is available on business models, including the components making up a business model (cf. Taran 2011) and frameworks of business models (Osterwalder *et al.* 2010), and still there seems to be a general consensus that no precise definition of a business model exists. According to Porter back in 2001 the definition of a business model was murky at best. Therefore, the theoretical grounding of most such business model definitions is still quite fragile despite the fact that at the present a substantial amount of literature is available on business models, including components, frameworks definitions etc. The aim of this chapter is to give an overview of existing definitions of a business model, and to provide frameworks for understandings of business models that are found in the literature. Fielt (2011) compares and categorizes a number of business model definitions below:

George & Bock (2009)	Morris et al. (2005)	Osterwalder et al.(2005)
organizational design	Economical level	activity/role-related approach
the resource-based view of the firm	Operational level	value/customer-oriented approach
narrative and sense-making	Strategic level	
the nature of innovation		
the nature of opportunity		
transactive structures		

Figure 7: Categorizations of business model definitions (Fielt 2011)

According to Osterwalder *et al.* 2004, a business model is a conceptual tool that contains "a set of elements and their relationships and allows expressing a company's logic of earning money. It is a description of the value a company offers to one or several segments of customers and the architecture of the firm and its network of partners for creating, marketing and delivering this value and relationship capital, in order to generate profitable and sustainable revenue stream". In this sense Osterwalder *et al.* here acknowledge that a business model to some extent becomes a mediating mechanism between the inside and the outside of the company.

Business model definitions and frameworks vary significantly according to whether they factor in outside relationships. Although the review here is structured around three types of perceptions of business models, these can only become crude classifications, as a great deal of overlap exists between business models and other concepts such as value chains and strategy. Thus, a clear interpretation of the boundaries of the review is a matter of interpretation. Here we have chosen to classify business model frameworks according to whether they concern generic descriptions of the business or whether they are more specific in their descriptions. The later category is divided according to whether the definitions solely consider elements inside the company (narrow) or also consider elements outside (broad).

The term generic business models, includes suggestions and definitions concentrating mainly on the elements such models ought to be comprised of in order to qualify as business models. On one hand this will provide an indication of which elements that could be considered necessary for the description of value creation from a business perspective, and on the other hand help differentiate business models from other related concepts and research areas such as supply chain management and organizational theory in general.

Next we focus on specific business models that are characterized by being more detailed than the generic business models, most often incorporating suggestions for specific elements or linkages; and often stating some kind of causality between the elements such as: activities, departments, processes or other. In the review we distinguish between broad specific business models that comprise focus on the whole enterprise system, including how the firm is positioned according to its partners in the value constellation, and narrow specific business models that focus on the specific, often causal, links between organizational activities, processes and the likes, and which do not consider external aspects.

It must also be admitted that the amount of literature referring to the business model concept has been almost exploding within the few years, so an exhaustive review is difficult. Figure 8 below illustrates this graphically, as the development in the number of published academic articles containing the term "business model" is depicted. Both of the article databases Ingenta and Emerald contain similar trends, starting from almost none in the mid-1990's to experiencing solid increases around the year 2000 and an explosion after 2005.

Year	Academic papers
2010	61070
2009	4573
2008	3238
2007	2462
2006	1976
2005	1505
2004	1325
2003	1098
2002	900
2001	659
>2000	598

Figure 8: Application of the term business model.

3.1.1 Generic business model definitions

Traditionally, business models have been associated with industry models, where certain factors are likely to improve the chance of success for an organization almost in such a way that "[t]he name of the industry served as shorthand for the prevailing business model's approach to market structure, organizational design, capital expenditures, and asset management" as Sandberg (2002, 3) provocatively states. This is for instance seen in the airline industry, where Hansson *et al.* (2002) illustrate how the traditional airline companies currently find themselves in a competitive situation where they must change their business models in order to remain profitable, and the pharmaceutical industry where Burcham (2000) accentuates that companies must acknowledge that information technology is changing not only their business models but the entire pharmaceutical value chain. Thus, from this perspective, the business model relates to general industry attributes. These industry attributes are at the same time determinative with respect to common organizational aspects, i.e. which components that constitute a profitable business in the respective sectors.

The weakness of an approach focussing mainly on industries is that changes, e.g. new technologies, often give rise to a new or updated version of the traditional business model.

Although of course there is a certain stability in the ways of doing business within specific industries, and despite the fact that industry structure to a great degree dictates which business models become profitable, our aim here is to move beyond a mere listing of industry types and associated business models. In the context of so-called highly turbulent and competitive business environments, Chaharbaghi *et al.* (2003) identify three interrelated strands which form the basis of a meta-model for business models: characteristics of the way of thinking in a company, its operational system, and capacity for value generation. Although being very general notions, three elements are expressible in more concrete terms. For instance, the characteristics of the way of thinking in a company essentially pertain to a strategic conception, while capacity for value generation is very much in line with a resource-based perspective. Finally, the element 'operational system' hints to the inclusion of processes and a value chain perspective.

Hedman & Kalling (2003) propose that a generic business model is composed of the causally related components: customers, competitors, the company offering (generic strategy), activities and organisation (including the value chain), resources (human, physical and organisational), and factor and production inputs. These notions are very much in line with Porter's (1991) causality chain model, which can be considered an account of a business model. Somewhat related to Porter's ideas are the recent suggestions relating to causal modelling of the service-profit-chain (Heskett *et al.* 1994) as a kind of general business model for the service sector.

Basing his ideas on the service management literature from the 1980's, Normann (2001) distinguishes between three different components of a generic business model: The external environment, the offering of the company and the internal factors such as organisational structure, resources, knowledge and capabilities. The first component is the external environment, its needs and what it is valuing. These characteristics are in turn prerequisites for the offering of the company, which is the second component. Finally we have internal factors such as organisational structure, resources, knowledge and capabilities, equipment, systems, leadership, and values which are necessary for the company to deliver its offering. In comparison to Hedman & Kalling, Normann goes one step further by implicating that the concept is systemic in nature, and that the relationship to the external environment depends on the offering, which in turn is dependent upon firm-internal factors.

In this manner, the generic typology constitutes a meta model or ontology for business models. According to Chaharbaghi *et al.* (2003), there are three interrelated strands forming the basis of such a meta-model for business models: characteristics of the way of thinking in the company, its operational system, and capacity for value generation. For instance, the characteristics of the way of thinking in the company essentially pertain to a strategic conception, while capacity for value generation is very much in line with a resource-based perspective.

Another terminology is chosen by Osterwalder & Pigneur (2003), who propose a business model 'ontology' which consists of four main pillars: product innovation, customer relationships, infrastructure management, and financial aspects. These can be further decomposed into their elements. This definition is very similar to the ideas spawned from Kraemer *et al.*'s study (1999), where the four building blocks of Dell's business model are identified as direct sales, direct customer relationships, customer segmentation for sales and service, and build-to-order production, as is also confirmed by Alt & Zimmermann (2001), who distinguish between six generic elements of a business model. The first three elements of Alt & Zimmermann's suggestion are recognizable: mission (including vision, strategic goals and value proposition), structure (value chain), and processes (activities, value creation processes). However, the latter three elements: revenues (bottom line), legal issues (e.g. regulation), and technology (impact on business model design) are new in this context. Betz (2002) also acknowledges the element of linking the various ideas of value offering, value creation etc. to the bottom line. He argues for the construction of a generic business model incorporating the four elements: resources, sales, profits and capital (See figure 9).

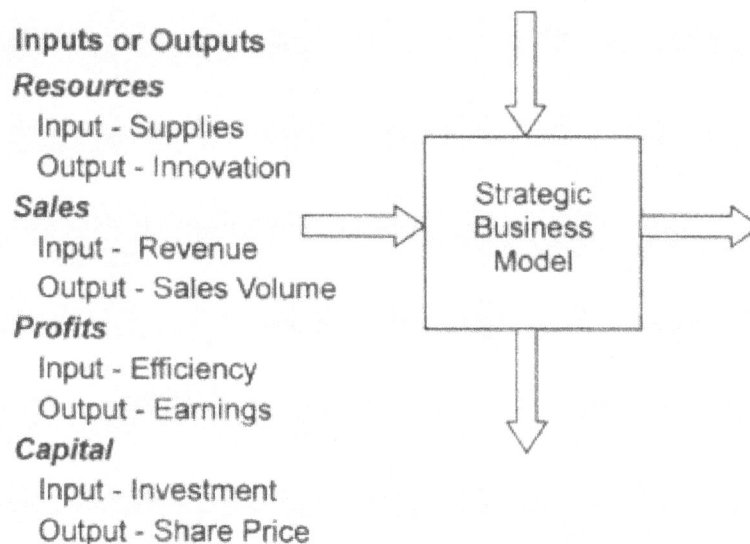

Inputs or Outputs

Resources
   Input - Supplies
   Output - Innovation
Sales
   Input - Revenue
   Output - Sales Volume
Profits
   Input - Efficiency
   Output - Earnings
Capital
   Input - Investment
   Output - Share Price

Strategic Business Model

Figure 9: Constructing a generic business model (Betz 2002, 22)

As can be seen from this brief review of the kind of business models that we here term generic business models, the characteristics are quite similar. However, the characteristics focussed on in the generic business models are, as could be expected, rather general and often encompassing the whole enterprise or value creating system (chain, network etc.).

3.1.2 Broad business model definitions

The first category of the specific business model definitions, i.e. business models that incorporate more precise suggestions with respect to the elements and linkages that enable value creation, is termed "broad" business models. In our terminology, this means that their focus is on the whole enterprise system, including how the firm is positioned according to its partners in the value constellation. As a general characteristic the broad models typically take a value chain perspective and include relationships to suppliers and customers while also taking external forces into account. Thereby in a sense also the concept of strategy.

A typical example of a broad business model understanding is Lev's (2001, 110) company 'fundamentals'. Drawing attention to Tasker's (1998) analysis of technology company conference calls, Lev emphasizes that the "information most relevant to decision making in the current economic environment concern the value chain of the enterprise (business model, in analysts' parlance)" (Lev 2001, 110; original emphasized).

However, Lev's definition of a business model takes its point of departure in Porter's (1985) classical notion of the value chain. Particularly, Lev states that by value chain he means "The fundamental economic process of innovation [...]that starts with the discovery of new products or services or processes [...] and culminates in the commercialization" (Lev 2001, 110). In a sense, this is a description of the architecture of the company for generating value, a notion quite similar to Afuah & Tucci (2000, 2) designating that a business model describes "how [the firm] plans to make money long-term".

According to Timmers (1998), a business model should be seen as "the architecture for the product, service and information flows, including a description of the various business actors and their roles; a description of the potential benefits for the various business actors; and a description of the sources of revenues." Timmers' definition is not very detailed and could probably also be categorized as a generic business model as the ones in the previous section. However, as it includes notions of visualizing how the business functions and a focus on the offering from the company to its customers, it relates as so more to the specific definitions.

A similar definition, in that it also has a focus on representation and value proposition is suggested by Weill & Vitale's (2001) who define a business model as, "a description of the roles and relationships among a firm's consumers, customers, allies and suppliers that identifies the major flows of product, information, and money, and the major benefits to participants". This too is a very broad definition, in essence covering all possible aspects of doing business.

A number of the definitions within this category have explicit reference to the term sustainable development. Sustainable development is in essence, the ability of the company to create revenue in the long-term, especially with consideration to the external stakeholders interests. Thus, there is a weak linkage to the generic definitions that often focuse more narrowly on profits and revenue, implicitly meaning a shorter term perspective.

Further, this way of conceptualizing the business model focuses on describing the method of doing business in a specific company. This is also in accordance with KPMG's definition of a business model as "The fundamental logic by which the enterprise creates sustained economic value – the organizations "business model" (KPMG 2001, 3, 11). The terms 'fundamental logic' and 'value configuration' resemble Stabell & Fjeldstad's value configuration logics (1998), and again these definitions cover all possible aspects of doing business.

Similarly, Rappa's definition (2001) states that "a business model is the method of doing business by which a company can sustain itself – that is, generate revenue. The business model spells-out how a company makes money by specifying its position in the value chain." As well as departing in the notion of sustainable development, it also incorporates a more specific notion of the position of the firm in the value chain.

Another suggestion that we will pay special attention to, is offered by Chesbrough & Rosenbloom (2002), who sees the business model as integrating a series of perspectives including strategy (Seddon *et al.* 2004), management (Magretta 2002b), innovation (Gaarder 2003), and e-business enabled distribution models among others, into "a coherent framework that takes technological characteristics and potentials as inputs, and converts them through customers and markets into economic outputs. The business model is thus conceived as a focusing device that mediates between technology development and economic value creation" (Chesbrough & Rosenbloom 2002, 5).

Although this understanding is developed specifically in relation to evidence from Xerox Corporations spin-off companies, the insights provided have a broader application and the authors also explicitly acknowledge "that firms need to understand the cognitive role of the business model, in order to commercialize technology in ways that will allow firms to capture value from their technology investments" (Chesbrough & Rosenbloom (2002, 5). The six components are discussed in greater detail in chapter 1.

These elements are representative for many authors' view on business models. According to Marrs & Mundt (2001), a business model is designed to compile, integrate, and convey information about the business and industry of an organization. Further, in the context of the so-called Strategic-Systems Auditing framework, Bell *et al.* (1997) identified six components of a business model: external forces, markets/formats, business processes, alliances, core products and services, and customers. In essence this framework focuses on describing "the interlinking activities carried out within a business entity, the external forces that bear upon the entity and the business relationships with persons and other organizations outside of the entity" (Bell *et al.* 1997, pp. 37-39).

Later Bell *et al.* (2002) developed these ideas in the direction of a value driver focus which is one of the characteristics dealt with in the next section. The notion of describing links and activities and processes is likewise emphasized by Weill & Vitale (2001), who define a business model as, "a description of the roles and relationships among a firm's consumers, customers, allies and suppliers that identifies the major flows of product, information, and money, and the major benefits to participants".

In comparison to the generic typology of business models, this broad specific understanding comes closer to treating 'how' the relationships are than merely 'what' objects should be included. Furthermore, the broad business models act as representation of the central roles and relationships of the firm, whereas the generic definitions were more focused on resources necessary for value creation.

3.1.3 Narrow business model definitions

In comparison to the category above, the narrow business model definitions are characterized by focusing only on internal aspects of the organization. As exponents of this view of the business model, Petrovic *et al.* (2001) argue that a business model ought not to be a description of a complex social system with all its actors, relations and processes, like the broad definitions imply. Instead, they contend, it should describe the value creating logic of a company (see also Linder & Cantrell 2002), the processes that enable this, i.e. the infrastructure for generating value, and constitute the foundation for conceptualizing the business strategy.

Similarly, Boulton *et al.* (2000) emphasize the need to create a business model that links combinations of assets to value creation. Having defined a business model as "[t]he unique combination of tangible and intangible assets that drives the ability of an organization to create or destroy value" (Boulton *et al.* 1997, 244), these authors' definitions can be seen as a detailed account of the internal prerequisites for value creation. Their focus on key measures of the value creation process, i.e. the value drivers, shows the uniqueness of internal aspects.

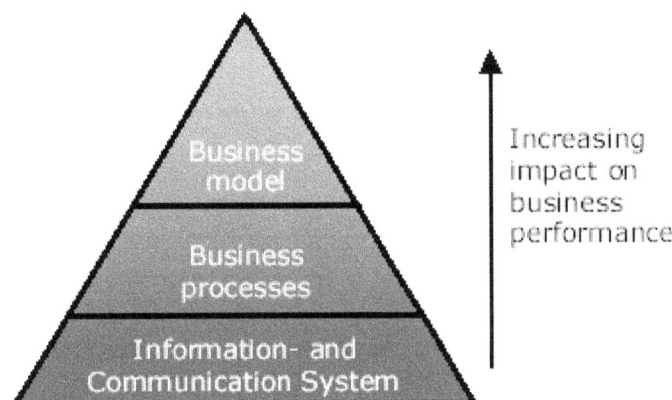

Figure 10: Hierarchical structure of business logic (Petrovic *et al.* 2001, 2)

Even more focused on value drivers and processes is Bray's view where "The business model is defined by the performance drivers, business processes, people and the infrastructure put in place to achieve the company's business objectives" (2002, 13). Bray's explicit link to business objectives is at the same a link to strategy and – especially – value creation, although this is not specifically stated. Value creation is, however, somewhat more explicitly mentioned in Linder & Cantrell's business model definition: "A real business model is the organization's core logic for creating value" (2002) as it more specifically

- The set of value propositions an organization offers to its stakeholders,
- Along with the operating processes to deliver on these,
- Arranged as a coherent system,
- That both relies on and builds assets, capabilities and relationships in order to create value.

Another central tool when describing a company's value creation story is to support narratives with non-financial performance measures. One thing is to state that one´s business model is based on mobilizing customer feedback in the innovation process, another thing is to explain by what means this will be done, and even more demanding is proving the effort by indicating: 1) how many resources the company devotes to this effort; 2) how active the company is in this matter, and whether it stays as focussed on the matter as initially announced; and 3) whether the effort has had any effect, e.g. on customer satisfaction, innovation output etc. According to Bray (2010, 6), "relevant KPIs measure progress towards the desired strategic outcomes and the performance of the business model. They comprise a balance of financial and non-financial measures across the whole business model.".

From this we can deduct that the business model should explain how the organization offers unique value, be hard to imitate, be grounded in reality (economics), and can help to ensure that different stakeholders are speaking the same language.

Competitive strategy is about being different, and the business model in this respect is the vehicle for operationalizing such differences. Thus, a well-constructed business model facilitates an understanding of the activities that really add value. A business model is thus an account of the links, processes, and networks of causes and effects that create value. Sandberg 2002 argues that a business model must identify the customers you want to serve, spell out how your business is different from all the others—its unique value proposition, explain how you will implement the value proposition, and finally also describe the profit patterns, the associated cash flows, and the attendant risks within the company.

In summary, the narrow definitions predominately focus on details regarding the internal prerequisites for profitability and business models as systems of representation. Some of the suggestions found in the literature also incorporate elements of value proposition and uniqueness. To conclude on this review of the different types of business model frameworks, the attributes of the three typologies of business model definitions along with possible strengths and weaknesses are listed in table 1 below.

Typology	Attributes	Possible strengths	Possible weaknesses
Generic business model definitions	• Components that constitute the business • General industry attributes • A meta model or ontology for business models	• The advantages of aggregation, i.e. gaining an understanding of the basics of the value creation in the company	• Picture conveyed becomes too general to convey anything relevant about the specific business
Broad business model definitions	• The method of doing business • Focus on the whole enterprise system • The architecture for generating value • Description of roles and relationships	• Value creation must be understood across the whole value chain in which the company participates	• Not sufficiently focused on the core value creating processes • Includes factors not completely controlled by the company
Narrow business model definitions	• Describe the uniqueness of internal aspects • Infrastructure for generating value • Detailed accounts of links, processes, and networks of causes and effects	• The level of detail regards the functioning of the specific firm • Precise and relevant descriptions	• Accounts may become too specific to make sense • Loss of overall understanding

Table 1: Attributes, strengths and weaknesses across the three typologies of business model definitions

3.2　Business model characteristics

The act of representing an object is equivalent to making it visible and thus manageable as when making activities auditable by representing accounting for them and when mechanisms are created to capture the essence of a phenomenon, e.g. in the representation of intellectual capital and value creation. Therefore, representation lies in the conception of the term business model itself. The business model – being a model of the business – is exactly such a representation, whether acknowledged explicitly or not. Focusing at the 'level of organizations', characterized by communication, interrelations, roles and division of labor etc., the system becomes as already Boulding (1956, 205) stated difficult to comprehend.

Simplifications needed because we as humans have limited cognitive abilities (Simon 1959). Representation is derivable as a question of how we transcribe the world around us for the sake of being able to comprehend it; in a sense perceiving representations as common-sense explanations of how objects are connected. Thus, we can perceive business models as representations of a business system where the specific business model in a company represents a choice between feasible alternatives (Chaharbaghi, Fendt & Willis, 2003) and essentially summarizes these choices that prepare the business to perform in the future (Betz 2002). Bell & Solomon (2002) enhance this perspective of the business model as a representation of the business system, in that it is a "simplified representation of the network of causes and effects that determine the extent to which the entity creates value", thereby underlining the business models role in illuminating the critical value drivers of the company.

Among the underlying notions of representation are concerns of objectivity, power, and description vs. transformation. As we, in this context, are interested in understanding how management can grasp the organization, i.e. conceptualize it and manage it, objectivity becomes a question of representational faithfulness (cf. Napier 1993).

As the first characteristic within this group we find perceptions of business models where the business model is seen as a representation of the business. Representation has several objectives and not just the obvious one of enabling conceptualization by creating a simplistic model of reality. As accentuated by Bell & Solomon (2002), management's ability to disperse their mental models through the organization and thereby create a common understanding of strategic direction, corporate culture etc. of the company is also a tool of power. This has some indications of a controlling-at-a-distance perspective (Cooper 1992). Chaharbaghi, Fendt & Willis (2003) accentuate this view and define business models as a representation of management thinking and practices that help businesses see, understand and run their activities in a distinct and specific way. Representation thus becomes a communicative tool in the sense of projection as the power to get ones projection out enables control from a distance.

When perceiving business models as simplified versions of reality, representation becomes an abstraction of the business, identifying how that business makes money. Business models are abstracts about how inputs to an organization are transformed to value-adding outputs (Betz 2002). Along these lines of thoughts, the business model functions as a construct (Chesbrough & Rosenbloom 2002), describing the relationships between the elements of the value creation system (Weill & Vitale 2001), illustrating e.g. the architecture of product, service and information flows (Timmers 1998).

Secondly, from a narrative perspective business models can be a support mechanism for projection of management's view to the organization through e.g. storytelling. The narrative perspective resembles a transformation/abbreviation perspective which in the end leads to the ability of remote control. Representation of the business through a description, i.e. a story of how it works (Magretta 2002) and the relationships it is engaged in. Very much in line with Hamel's (2000) ideas, Morris (2003) conceptualizes the business model as a "comprehensive description of business." A business model, according to Morris, is therefore a description of a whole system, including how the experiences of creating and delivering value may evolve along with the changing needs and preferences of customers (Morris 2003, 17).

Key aspects of narrative-focused business model definitions are: description, stories, expression and explanation, like e.g. Sandberg states, "business models describe and explain" (2002, 4) or "stories that explain how enterprises work" (Magretta 2002a, 4). For example, they can explain how you will implement the value proposition like the knowledge narrative of an intellectual capital statement (Mouritsen *et al.* 2003).

Finally, the business model can be seen as facilitating understanding accentuates the business model as a management technology, which can help management in explaining and comprehending aspects of how the company functions. Being able to speak the same 'language' throughout the entire organization is an enormous feat to achieve. "Imagine a world where employees understood what it takes for their company to make money" as Linder & Cantrell (2002) say. Facilitating understanding therefore works through abbreviation, i.e. as a simplification-mechanism, enhancing the bounded rationality perspective on human action.

The use of a business model approach to helps management communicate and share their understanding of the business logic to stakeholders, i.e. capital market agents such as analysts and investors. The external reporting of the value creation logic of the business provides a way of analyzing the prospects of the firm by creating a mutual understanding, in a sense advocating for business models being able to serve as a new unit of analysis.

Among the key aspects addressed in connection with business models from the perspective of facilitating understanding is creating a mutual understanding, e.g. between company management and capital market agents, but also to create a common understanding of a business model for all actors involved, and to assess the potential profitability of a business model. Modeling the business also offers the capability to map out new business ideas graphically in a clear and communicable fashion, so that the conceptualization will allow the understanding of, and reasoning behind the underlying business idea. This can be achieved by using one or more of the frameworks presented in chapter 5 of this book.

Business models are perhaps a more comprehensive way of understanding the focus of competition merely trying to conceptualize strategy. The notion here is to explain the company's unique value proposition to external parties, as Sandberg (2002) states: "Spell out how your business is different from all the others." Finally, the facilitating understanding perspective is not solely to be thought of as an external communication aspect. The mere process of modeling the business helps management in identifying and understanding the relevant elements of their business (Osterwalder & Pigneur 2003), like e.g. value drivers and other causal relationships.

This section reviews the parts of the literature that have been found representative or most relevant in developing the frameworks of a business model. Table 2 below illustrates the structure chosen for the review. In the literature reviewed, 9 subunits of characteristics that are emphasized as integral parts of a business model are discussed. These areas, which are termed 'characteristics of business models' have, for simplicity, been grouped into three archetypes of categories: (1) what the overall purpose of the firm or the criteria for success is, (2) what kind of elements are important and (3) how these elements interrelate.

1	**The overall criteria for performance**	Sustainable development
		Strategy
		Improving the business and innovation
2	**The elements of the business model**	Resource-base
		Value chain
		Value proposition
3	**Relationships between elements**	Value drivers
		Value creation
		Causal relationships

Table 2: Overview of business model characteristics

3.2.1 The overall criteria for performance

While the ultimate goal of a company from a shareholder perspective is to create profits, business models sometimes address broader criteria such as sustainable development, which implies that focus is shifted from mere profit orientation towards sustainable enterprises and an economic reality that connects industry, society and the environment. This need for linking sustainable development to business strategy is, for instance, acknowledged by Funk (2003, 65), who characterizes the sustainable organization as "one whose characteristics and actions are designed to lead to a 'desirable future state' for all stakeholders", and by Afuah & Tucci (2000), who argue that the business model concerns sustainable development through the firm's unique value configuration which is synonymous with KPMG's definition of the business model as: "The fundamental logic by which the enterprise creates sustained economic value – the organization's business model" (KPMG 2001, 11).

In recent years there has been increased attention to reporting on sustainable development within the business reporting debate, e.g. triple bottom line reporting (Elkington 1997) and the Global Reporting Initiative (GRI 2010). Non-accounting information such as forward-looking sustainability indicators are, in line with intangibles becoming a greater part of wealth creation, becoming more relevant to the overall value proposition of a business. In this sense the business model becomes a central notion, as it is the method of doing business by which a company can sustain itself, that is, generate revenue.

In using the notion of a business model as our key concept, we therefore implicitly assume that it comprehends something more than strategy and more than profits, or at least is a concept different from merely treating strategy and profits. In this sense Magretta (2002, 6) is clear when she states that "business models describe, as a system, how the pieces of a business fit together. But they don't factor in one critical dimension: competition", which implies that she finds the competitive basis of the companies to be completely outside the business model.

Another perspective is offered by Czuchry & Yasin (2003), who argue that a business model is not necessarily successful by itself, because firms must integrate and align strategic and operational efforts, activities, resources and decisions into a systematic organizational strategy, thus indicating that strategy is an integrated component of a business model. A different angle to this discussion comes from Chesbrough & Rosenbloom (2001, 535), who argue that while business models are more oriented towards value creation and sustainable development from a bounded rationality perspective, strategy theory is more apt to consider value creation from a shareholder perspective and to suppose full analytical rationality of decision-makers.

Also Seddon *et al.* (2004) studies the relationship between strategy and business models and conclude that strategies are grounded in the real world, whereas business models are abstractions of the real-world strategies of the companies. Likewise, with regard to improving corporate performance measures to drive results and very much in line with Kaplan & Norton's thoughts of the balanced scorecard (1992; cf. Eccles 1991). Also, Miller, Eisenstat & Foote (2002) perceives the business model as a means of linking measurements to strategies. Actually, Sandberg (2002), referring to Porter's (1996) articulations on competitive strategy about being different, argues that the business model is the vehicle for operationalizing those differences. Therefore, although not the same, there is a positive mutually supporting interrelation between business models and strategy (Heinrichs & Lim 2003).

Finally, business models have, as our third characteristic, also been associated with the efforts of companies to improve the business and innovate. Much early literature (cf. Kodama 1999) takes its point of departure in how new technology, most notably the Internet, has revolutionized certain industries and changed the feasibility of existing business models. This is, for instance, illustrated by Gallaugher (2002), who shows how e-commerce has enabled the emergence of new business models.

Following Hamel & Skarzynski (2001), innovation can be perceived as the route to wealth creation but is also a prerequisite for sustainable development because today's competitive advantage becomes tomorrow's albatross as Christensen (2001) has expressed it. Having the right business model at the present doesn't necessarily guarantee success for years on end. Causes can be new technology but also changes in the environment and the customer base can play a role (Delmar 2003) as is illustrated by the European airline Ryanair which has with great success significantly restructured the business model of the airline industry. As the air transport markets have matured, incumbent companies that have developed sophisticated and complex business models now face tremendous pressure to find less costly approaches that meet broad customer needs with minimal complexity in products and processes (Hansson, Ringbeck & Franke 2002).

Other authors that draw attention to need for business model innovation and renewal are Sull (1999, 42) and De Carolis (2003, 44) who ask the dire question of what happens when companies fail to renew their business model as well as Ross, Weill & Vitale (2001) who pose the question of how to ensure that management will acknowledge that the existing business model is not profitable and change it.

Very often radical strategy changes means changing the entire business model (Upton & McAffe, 2000). Thus Govindarajan & Gupta (2001) link the business model with innovation by applying a business model perspective to strategic innovation. They identify three areas for changing the existing business: redesigning the architecture of the value chain, reinventing the concept of customer value, or redefining the customer base. This is basically strategic positioning in terms of value creation; what, how, and to whom (Markides 1997).

Kartseva, Gordijn & Akkermans (2003) suggest applying a business model as the basis for strategic analysis since this offers the possibility for mapping new business ideas graphically in a clear and communicable fashion. In this way business models facilitate change because of their building-block-like approach to formulating the business logic of a company (Petrovic *et al.* 2001). Chaharbaghi, Fendt & Willis accentuate this by stating that "the context-dependency of the specific business models provides the power of description and prescription, helping businesses see, understand and run their activities in a distinct way" (2003, 381) and Morris (2003, 25) confides that since business models are a more comprehensive way of understanding the focus of competition, they must also be the focus of innovation. Relentlessly changing conditions means that business models evolve rapidly and business model innovation is therefore not optional, rather it becomes mandatory. While innovations in any area within an organization may be important, innovations that pertain broadly and directly to the business model will be life-sustaining. Even the best-designed business model cannot last forever but must keep pace with shifting customer needs, markets and competitive threats (Linder & Cantrell 2002).

3.2.2 Performance related elements

In this section we take a closer look at how business models describe elements of the organization which are a part of the performance of the company. Performance related elements are elements that relate to the actual structure of the company. We distinguish between three characteristics that are labeled 'resource-base', 'value-chain' and 'value proposition'. The resource-base in the company is important, as there has been a lot of focus on which resources actually drive company value creation. For example, in the knowledge society it is stated that primarily knowledge drives value creation. Along these lines, Miller, Eisenstat & Foote (2002) argue that capabilities are the backbone of the competitive advantage of a company, because such resources constitute a more stable element on which to base sustainable development than competitive strategy in a highly volatile business environment. Confirming this, De Carolis (2003) finds that imitability of firm knowledge resources has a significant negative effect on firm performance. In a business environment characterized by rapid and discontinuous nature of change a framework that can facilitate business model innovation becomes necessary for sustainable competitive advantage (Malhotra 1999).

As resources are central aspects of a generic business model framework (Betz 2002) the resource-based view is appropriate in connection with business models (Hedman & Kalling 2003). Klaila (2000) explains how the business model helps to identify the critical behaviors, competencies, and market conditions and account for the resources of intellectual capital in the company. From the resource-based perspective we must perceive resources in the sense of being assets (Boulton *et al.* 1997) and inputs to the value creation process of the company. As it is difficult for organizations to understand the role of knowledge resources in their value creation (Covin & Stivers, 1997) the business model approach becomes advantageous by visualizing the capability configurations of the company, which are the cohesive combination of resources and capabilities embedded within its infrastructure that generate value (Miller, Eisenstat & Foote, 2002).

Porter defines the value chain as a basic tool for analyzing the sources of competitive advantage of the firm. The value chain enables a systematic examination of all the activities a firm performs and how these activities interact (1985, 33). Every firm is essentially a collection of interdependent activities that are performed to create value. According to Shank and Govindarajan (1992), the value chain can also be perceived as a generic concept for organizing our thinking about strategic positioning. They define the value chain as "the linked set of value-creating activities all the way from basic raw materials to the ultimate end-use product delivered into the final consumers' hands" (ibid., 179).

Within the notions of business models, the value chain comprises the activities and organization of the company (Hedman & Kalling 2001) and the structure of the company (Alt & Zimmermann 2001). In Bell *et al.*'s (1997) framework, core business processes and activities, and the analysis hereof, are viewed in the light of a value chain perspective. Likewise, Chesbrough & Rosenbloom (2002) imply that the value chain perspective leads to identification of the activities and assets (inputs) that are necessary to deliver the value proposition of the company (outputs). In this sense the business model spells out how a company makes money by specifying where it is positioned in the value chain (Rappa 2001).

However, there are alternative value configuration models to that of the value chain. Stabell & Fjeldstad (1998, 414) suggest that the value chain is but one of three generic value configuration models. Based on Thompson's (1967) typology of long-linked, intensive and mediating technologies, they define the value chain as a value configuration that models the activities of long-linked technology. Stabell & Fjeldstad (1998), in distinguishing between these three distinct generic value configuration models, argue that such a distinction is required in order to create an understanding and ultimately facilitate the analysis of firm-level value creation across a broad range of industries and firms.

The first of the two alternative generic value configuration models proposed by Stabell & Fjeldstad (1998) is the value shop logic. It concerns firms where value is created by mobilizing resources and activities to resolve a particular customer problem. The second alternative to the value chain is the value network logic. It models firms that create value by facilitating a network relationship between their customers using a mediating technology, e.g. like an infomediary or innomediary, as Sawhney *et al.* (2003) explicates.

According to Giertz (2000), each type of business is based on such unique value creation logic. Understanding and managing companies, he argues, thus requires a simulation that will test the business model and its strategy. Referring to Stabell & Fjeldstad, this would incorporate identifying the applied value configuration or business logic, and development of appropriate performance measures, as accentuated by Eccles (1991) and Kaplan & Norton (2008).

Along these lines, Allee (2000) contends that in order to facilitate the analysis of the value of such networks, knowledge and intangible value exchanges must become an integrated part of the business models applied in visualizing these new value configurations. In this connection, Hamel (2000) talks of competing value networks – a synonym for the inter-corporate value chain and Porter's value system – which, as we will see later on is an important aspect of distinguishing between different types of business models (2000, 88).

Sweet (2001) identifies four strategic value configuration logics: value-adding, -extracting, -capturing, and -creating, that exist no matter the prevailing macroeconomic paradigm.

Sweet argues that it is the ability to manage these logics well that creates success rather than new business models. By stating this, he confirms the necessity of understanding how the business model and its value creating elements work, as a prerequisite for managing the company. Ramirez (1999) too, offers an alternative view to that associated with value creation in industrial production, arguing that technical breakthroughs and social innovations in actual value creation render the alternative, a so-called value co-production framework. This is also an alternative value configuration in line with the notions presented above by Stabell & Fjeldstad (1998) and Sweet (2001).

The value proposition or offering of the company depicts which value it intends to deliver to its customers. "A 'business model' is [...] a precise definition of who customers are, and how the company intends to satisfy their needs both today and tomorrow" (Morris 2003, 19). Morris' definition, which takes its point of departure in the value of the offering to the end users by the company, is very close to the definition of the knowledge narrative from the Danish guideline for intellectual capital statements. The knowledge narrative "expresses the company's ambition to increase the value a user receives from a company's goods or services" (Mouritsen *et al.* 2003a, 12).

Chesbrough & Rosenbloom (2002) similarly define the value proposition as the value created for the user of the offering from the company. Webb & Gile (2001) reject the notion of customer needs being the only true strategic approach and thereby argue against the previous literature, which state that the resources of the company ought to be the starting point of strategy formulation. For Hedman & Kalling (2001) the value proposition of the company is equivalent to the generic strategy of the company. In a likewise manner, Alt & Zimmermann (2001) define the value proposition as a part of the mission statement of the company together with its vision and strategic goals. Each type of business has its unique value proposition logic (Giertz 2000) as the value proposition is closely linked to the products and services delivered. Osterwalder & Pigneur (2003) equivocate the value proposition with product innovation. Therefore it is a dire necessity to spell out how your business is different from all the others, i.e. your unique value proposition, and explain how you intend to implement the value proposition (Sandberg 2002).

3.2.3 Relationships between elements

The final category of business model characteristics concerns descriptions of internal linkages in the company related to performance and creating value. By relationships between elements we mean aspects such as value drivers, value creation processes and causality between e.g. activities, resources, and processes. These three categories regard the internal aspects of the business model of a company because they all are concerned with value creation. Value drivers will vary significantly by industry, or should we say by business model. Regardless of industry, it is of vital importance for a company to understand the drivers behind its value creation (Fenigstein 2003), i.e. which aspects deliver value-added? However, value drivers will vary significantly by industry, or should we say by business model. Value drivers are typically performance measurements with regard to core processes.

Understanding the value drivers of a company leads to the identification of key performance indicators. Bray (2002) perceives value drivers as the link between key performance indicators and business objectives, at the same time underlining that value drivers are not outcome-oriented key performance indicators, rather they are forward oriented performance measures. Hedman & Kalling (2003) propose value drivers as measurements of actual activity, which they state is an intermediary level separating the resources and the offering of the company. As value drivers imply causal relationships, they are more clearly visualized in a business model.

In Bell *et al.*'s framework (1997), value drivers are not explicitly mentioned, but can be viewed as the interlinking of specific activities performed in the core business processes of the company. As depicted above, key performance indicators are, according to Bray (2002), linked to business objectives via identification of the key drivers of value, which in turn can be interpreted as key success factors. Value drivers are not static performance measures, they will vary over time, both within a business cycle and from business cycle to business cycle (Wahlström 2003), and eventually the present value-drivers of the company will be replaced. This may be a result of the company changing its strategy or business model, which must have an effect on the drivers involved in the value chain and value creation process, or it could be an effect of the changing external environment.

A business model is inevitably a representation of how the company creates value, and value creation, therefore, is a cornerstone of the business model concept. The external prerequisite, the value proposition, is a central notion when referring to the internal prerequisite value creation, as the offering of the firm affects the value it must create and deliver to its customers and the users of its products or services. A business model thus depicts the design of transaction content, structure, and governance so as to create value through the exploitation of business opportunities (Amit & Zott 2001).

According to Linder & Cantrell (2002, 1), "a real business model is the organization's core logic for creating value". In fact the entire enterprise is a value creation system within which assets tangible as well as intangible are utilized and created. In this process, it is important to develop a strategy for bundling all the sources of value creation potential in a company into a single "recipe for adding value" (Daum 2002), i.e. a business model. Alt & Zimmermann (2001) also link the business model to value creation, by stating that it describes the logic that lies behind the actual processes of a 'business system' for creating value.

The ability of establishing precise connections and causal links and relationships between knowledge resources, competences, intellectual capital etc. and the value creation of an organization has been in the interest of the business and academic communities for a long time. Furthermore, it is an important element of the business model approach (Hedman & Kalling 2003). However, this relationship may be an unsettled one. Hermans' (2002) research within the context of Finnish biotechnology firms provides an exception. He tests and analyzes empirically how intellectual capital is connected to the market potential of Finnish biotechnology firms, finding among other things that management experience, research and patent application intensities, and the public financing of R&D activities have significant influence on growth prospects of the enterprises.

The ability to establish causal links between resources, activities, processes and their outcomes, i.e. value, is a prime deliverable of applying a business model perspective. It ensures that what is being measured is relevant, an argument that has been aired previously by the likes of Kaplan & Norton (2001) and Ittner & Larcker (1998). According to Dikolli & Kulp (2003), this business model approach to performance measurement helps identify and focus on the causal links between managerial actions, intermediate performance measures, and overall firm performance. Via a business model approach it is possible to identify causal loops that depict linkages between key performance measures and financial results (Bell *et al.* 1997) and which link combinations of assets to value creation (Boulton *et al.* 1997).

In relation to the overall perspective of the book, the characteristics and elements making up a business model, as identified above, can be viewed as proxies for the characteristics that constitute the fundamental mosaic of the market for information participants. In that respect, these aspects and elements indicate which types of information further studies should focus on in relation to gaining a better understanding of this mystery mosaic that informs financial numbers and the valuation of companies.

3.3   Towards business model building blocks

Several recent studies conduct comparisons of business model building blocks. Whiel Fielt (2011) focuses on the building blocks of e-business models, Taran (2011) looks at a broader selection of texts. The table below illustrates Taran's analysis from the perspective of Osterwalder & Pigneurs Business Model Canvas. It conveys a comparison between Osterwalder & Pigneur's 9 building blocks and Chesbrough's (2006) and Morris *et al.*'s (2003) 6 components. This table illustrates neatly the overlap between the models and the blanks. Taran concludes his review by using the 5 building blocks in the left hand column as a basis for suggesting a slightly rearranged model with 7 building blocks. See chapter 7 for more detail on this split. This is depicted in figure 11 below.

	Building Block	Description	Chesbrough 2006	Morris et al. 2003
Product	Value Proposition	Gives an overall view of a company's bundle of products and services	Component 1: Articulate the value of the proposed offering	Component 1: Factors related to offering
Customer Interface	Target Customer	Describes the segments of customers a company wants to offer value to	Component 2: Identify the market segment	Component 2: Market factors
	Distribution Channel	Describes the company's various means of getting in touch with its customers	Component 3: Define the value chain to deliver that offering	-
	Relationship	Explains the kind of links a company establishes between itself and its different customer segments	-	-
Infrastructure Management	Value Configuration	Describes the arrangement of activities and resources	Component 3: Define the value chain to deliver that offering	Component 3: Internal capability factors
	Core Competence	Outlines the competences necessary to execute the company's business model	-	Component 3: Internal capability factors
	Partner Network	Portrays the network of cooperative agreements with other companies necessary to efficiently offer and commercialize value	Component 3: Define the value chain to deliver that offering Components 5: Describe the position of the firm within the value network	-
Financial Aspects	Cost Structure	Sums up the monetary consequences of the means employed in the business model	Component 4: Establish cost structure and profit potential	Component 5: Economic factors
	Revenue Model	Describes the way a company makes money through a variety of revenue stream	Component 4: Establish cost structure and profit potential	Component 5: Economic factors
Strategy Aspects	Competitive Factor	-	Component 6: Formulate a competitive strategy	Component 4: Competitive strategy factor Component 6: Growth/exit factors

Figure 11: Break-down of business model building blocks (Taran 2011)

Sum-up questions for chapter 3

- What is the difference between a broad business model definition and a narrow business model definition?
- How does a generic business model definition differ from the above?
- Which overall characteristics of business model definitions can be identified
- What is the purpose of distinguishing business models on the terms of their overall characteristics?
- Discuss the interrelations between the building blocks set out in figure 11
- What are the interrelations between business model characteristics and business model building blocks?

4 Frameworks for understanding and describing business models

This chapter provides in a chronological fashion an introduction to six frameworks that one can apply to describing, understanding and also potentially innovating business models. These six frameworks have been chosen carefully as they represent six very different perspectives on business models and in this manner "complement" each other. There are a multitude of varying frameworks that could be chosen from and we urge the reader to search and trial these for themselves. The six chosen models (year of release in parenthesis) are:

- Service-Profit Chain (1994)
- Strategic Systems Auditing (1997)
- Strategy Maps (2001)
- Intellectual Capital Statements (2003)
- Chesbrough's framework for Open Business Models (2006)
- Business Model Canvas (2008)

4.1   Service-profit chain

While the concept of the Service-Profit Chain is relatively unknown in the accounting, finance and innovation literature, it is more well-known in marketing management. This concept was first offered in 1994 and is heavily skewed towards a commercial reality in which the customer service of the company is assumed to portend the future for a growing number of businesses. Originally developed as a marketing management tool, the Service-Profit Chain observes that, in the "new economics of service", senior management needs to focus on employees and customers rather than on profit goals and market share (Heskett *et al.* 1994). This logic is not dissimilar to that of Kaplan & Norton's strategy maps (see section below) where the desired value manifests itself in high levels of profitability and increased market share is created by a workforce that is satisfied and loyal. Consequently, the positive attitude of employees is essential because these are the individuals who deliver the service to customers on a face-to-face basis. Even in the case of exemplary levels of service provision, a degree of customer turnover is unavoidable as individuals find their personal circumstances change, however, ways of minimizing such leakages become another strategic priority.

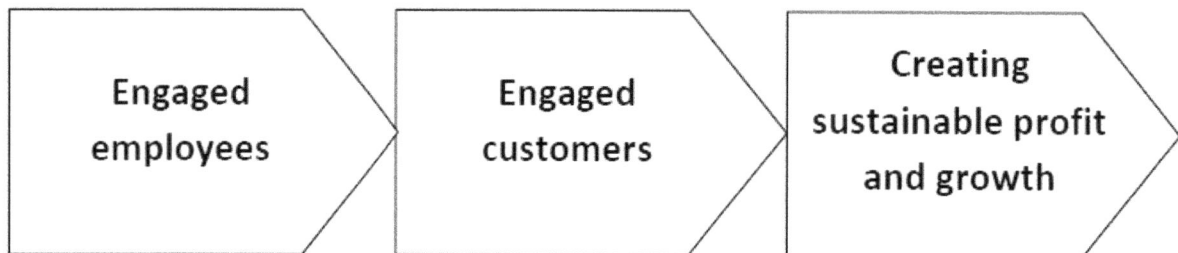

Figure 12: The Service-Profit Chain

The Service-Profit Chain is presented as a horizontal visualisation, with employee satisfaction identified using various attributes including: workplace design; job design; employee selection and development; employee rewards and recognition; and the provision of the necessary "tools for serving customers". Implicit here is the requirement for all of these attributes to be embedded, reproduced and enhanced on a continuous basis. The immediate outcomes of high levels of employee satisfaction are then identified as employee loyalty and retention, both of which impact on a preparedness to strive for the highest levels of customer service provision. The latter are identified as the key to high levels of customer satisfaction and loyalty. Success in this regard is linked to high levels of customer retention, which Heskett *et al.* associate with zero customer defections (see Reichheld & Sasser Jr, 1990). Beyond simply retaining customers, opportunities for cultivating the advocacy of service offerings should constantly be explored.

Consequently, the Service-Profit Chain identifies a wide range of measurement metrics that may be used to report the performance of a business. As with the Strategy Map concept, a scoreboard is used to report company performance with a strong emphasis on employee and customer metrics and rather less on the actual business process. Conventional financial performance indicators also have a place within such a scoreboard approach but, as Heskett *et al.* observe, their importance is decentred. Thus, the approach provides the opportunity to combine sets of relevant lead (forward-looking) and lag (historical) indicators. Finally, the Service-Profit Chain uses narrative reporting to complement numbers and the focus on employees and customers, are best served by the use of more qualitative forms of reporting, which in turn complement the underlying strategy narrative.

In the Service-Profit Chain literature we find hints that the growing emphasis on businesses to produce year-on-year increases in shareholder value has had a negative impact on the evolution of the long-term evolution of the company. The Service-Profit Chain is in this sense a horizontal representation that begins with a market overview, which informs the business strategy. The business strategy translates into a range of value creating activities, including "customers" and "people". The expectation is that, if appropriate sustainable relationships are maintained between the company and its customers and staff, long term financial performance will ensue.

4.2 The strategic systems auditing framework

Remembering that the business model is the platform which enables the strategic choices to become profitable, then it is clear that a business model is not a pricing strategy, a new distribution channel, an information technology, nor is it a quality control scheme in the production setup. A business model is concerned with the value proposition of the company, but it is not the value proposition alone as in itself it is supported by a number of parameters and characteristics. The question is here: how is the strategy and value proposition of the company leveraged?

To understand the foundations of the business model, metaphorically speaking, the pillars on which the platform rests, it is necessary to look at the organizational attributes of the company. In doing so, the focus should not be on the elements themselves, i.e. organizational structure, alliances, management processes, customer types, but rather on the characteristics of the links between them. A few years after the Service-Profit Chain came out of the marketing management literature, the collaboration between KPMG and a group of financial reporting and auditing researchers and University of Illinois – Urbana Champagne, gave birth to the "Client Business Model" as it was called by KPMG. By the involved researchers it was denoted the Strategic Systems Auditing framework (henceforth the SSA framework).

Bell *et al.* define "The (client) business model as a strategic-systems decision frame that describes the interlinking activities carried out within a business entity, the external forces that bear upon the entity, and the business relationships with persons and other organizations outside of the entity" (1997, pp. 37-39). As such they identify six components which need to be described in order to encompass the description of a business model:

- External forces
- Markets
- Business processes
    o Strategic management process
    o Core business processes
    o Resource management processes
- Alliances
- Core products and services
- Customers.

Bell *et al.* (1997) reason that gaining an understanding of key value creation processes and related competencies that enable the company to realize its strategy is an essential element of understanding its financial figures. By measuring and benchmarking the performance of core business processes and management and support processes, the 'KPMG Business Measurement Process', depicted in figure 13 below, facilitates and enhances an understanding of the risks that threaten attainment of the business objectives of the company. The following of this framework is argued to lead to an understanding of client business model and a documentation the ability of the company to create value and generate future cash flows, through depiction of the specific process analyses, key performance indicators, and business risk profile in the specific company, thus a similar procedure could potentially form the foundation for external communication more generally.

The KPMG Business Measurement Process

Continuous Improvement
Gaps and Opportunities

Driver · Systems · Driver

Strategic Analysis	Business Process Analysis	Business Measurement
External Forces	Strategic Management	Performance
Markets		Financial
Alliances	Core Business Processes	Market
Products	Resource Management Processes	Process
Customers		Resource

Risk Assessment
Business Risks and Controls

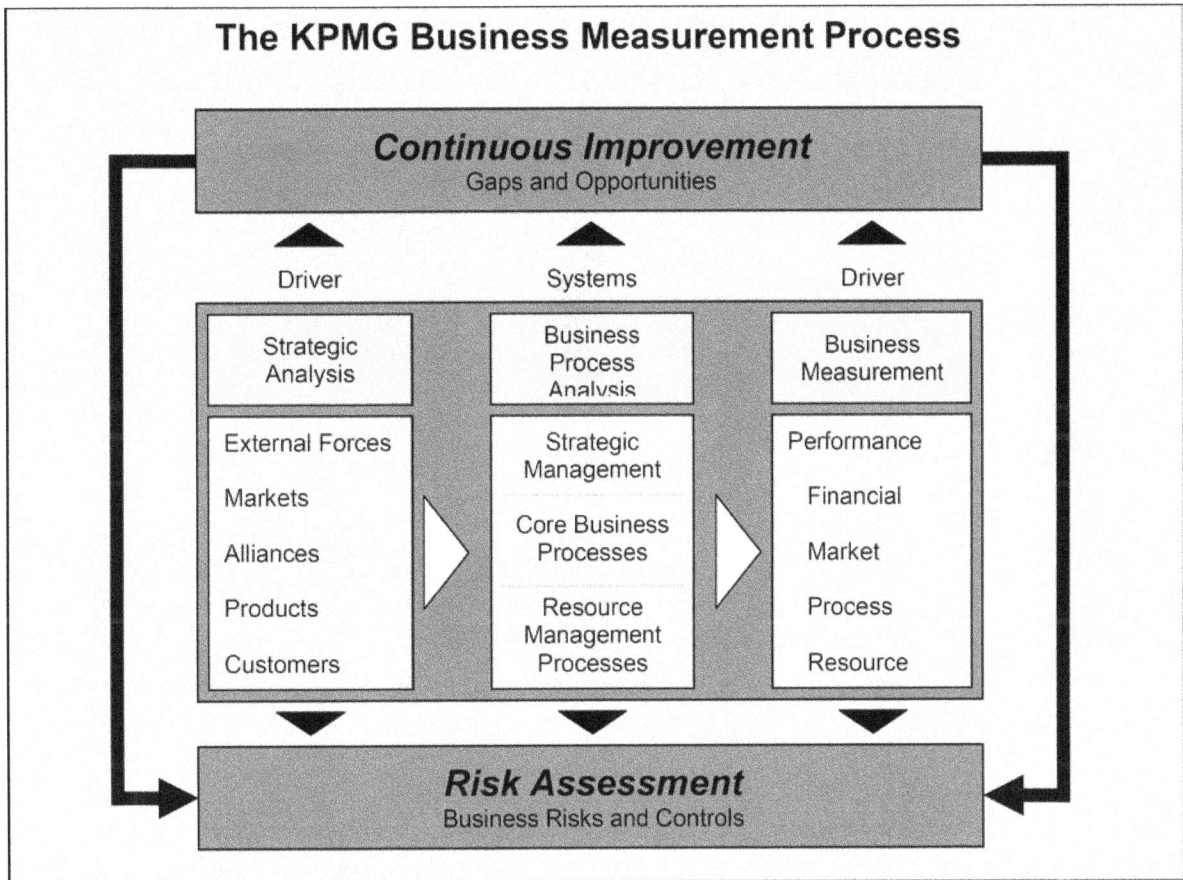

Figure 13: The KPMG Business Measurement Process (Bell *et al.* 1997)

The SSA model is as such based on an analysis procedure that departs in the strategic analysis of the external forces affecting the company, the markets on which it operates, along with an analysis of its alliances, products, and customers. Next, an analysis of the business processes regarding strategic management processes, core business processes, and resource management processes leads to a so-called Entity Level Business Model and the identification of key business performance measures. This is depicted in figure 14 below.

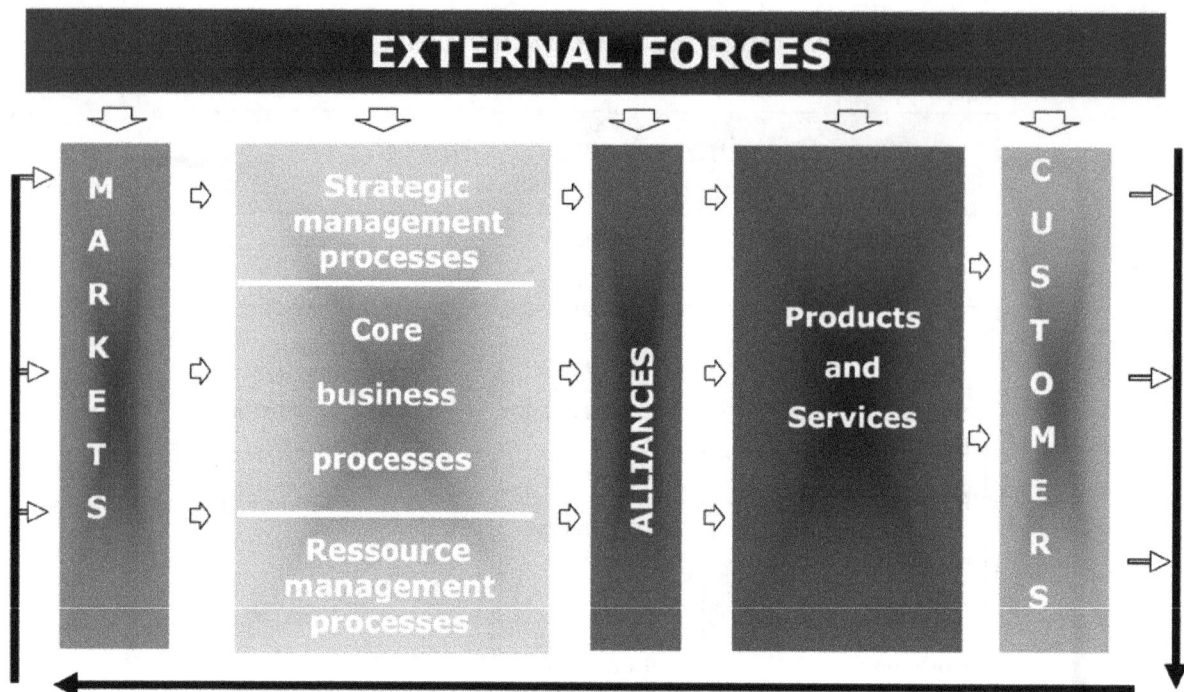

EXTERNAL FORCES

M A R K E T S

Strategic management processes

Core business processes

Ressource management processes

ALLIANCES

Products and Services

C U S T O M E R S

Figure 14: The Client business model (Bell *et al.* 1997)

Following up on the Strategic-Systems Auditing (SSA) model, Bell & Solomon define the business model as: "a simplified representation of the network of causes and effects that determine the extent to which the entity creates value and earns profits" (2002, xi). An interesting catch here is the distinction between value creation and profits, instigating that value creation should be perceived from a broader perspective than merely a shareholder value perspective.

Compared to the suggestions by Bell *et al.* (1997), the 2002 framework provided by Bell & Solomon focuses more narrowly on value creation and has predominately internal focus incorporating the elements of value drivers, value creation, and representation. As a distinctive feature, the SSA model departs from an auditing perspective where Bell *et al.* (1997) argue for the importance of gaining an understanding of the client's strategic advantage. This is, however, not only a necessity from an auditing perspective since understanding the strategic advantage of a company is the prerequisite for understanding how it creates value.

Gaining an understanding of key value creation processes and related competencies that enable the company to realize its strategy is an essential element of such an analysis. By measuring and benchmarking the performance of core business, management and support processes, the 'KPMG Business Measurement Process', depicted in figure 13, facilitates and enhances an understanding of the risks that threaten the attainment of the business objectives in the company. The following of this framework is argued to lead to an understanding of the client's business model and a documentation of the ability of the company to create value and generate future cash flows through depiction of the specific process analyses, key performance indicators, and business risk profile in the specific company. Thus, a similar procedure could potentially form the foundation for external communication more generally.

The SSA model is based on an analysis procedure that departs in the strategic analysis of the external forces affecting the company and the markets on which it operates, along with an analysis of its alliances, products, and customers. Next, an analysis of the business processes regarding strategic management processes, core business processes, and resource management processes leads to a so-called Entity Level Business Model and the identification of key business performance measures.

SSA gives an idea of the parameters that make up and define the outskirts of a business model. Through the strategic analysis, the following aspects of the organization are described: external forces, markets, alliances, products, and customers. Next, the SSA model includes a process analysis tool which helps the analyst from a risk based perspective to find the most appropriate KPI's and controls of key risks for the company to be able to deliver the value proposition and through this identify the characteristics and key aspects of the links between organizational elements. The business process analysis is applied on three archetypes of processes, namely: strategic management processes, core business processes, and resource management processes. The process analysis follows the steps depicted below:

1. Process objectives
2. Inputs
3. Activities
4. Outputs
5. Systems
6. Classes of transactions
7. Risks which threaten objectives
8. Critical success factors
9. Other symptoms of poor performance
10. Performance improvement opportunities

Finally, the step of identifying Critical Success Factors leads to the actual business performance measurement including the identification of performance KPI's according to the four dimensions: financial, market, process, and resource. This process is illustrated in the box below for a Merger & Acquisition choice process.

4.3 Strategy maps

The Strategy Map (Kaplan & Norton, 2001; 2004) is a development of the Balanced Scorecard which originally emerged from management accounting practices in the mid 1980s (Kaplan and Norton, 1992, 1993; see also Maisel, 1992). Initially, the Balanced Scorecard was described as a multi-perspective reporting framework; its principal function was to enhance internal management reporting, however, it was later considered to also have potential for external reporting. Kaplan & Norton (1992) identified four generic perspectives for the Balanced Scorecard: growth and development (later learning and growth); internal business processes; the customer; and financial perspectives. They later asserted that these four perspectives could be viewed as forming a cause and effect chain that was represented as a vertical configuration beginning with the learning and growth perspective Kaplan & Norton, 1996). As learning and growth is developed within a company, upward links are made to the internal (business process) perspective. Business processes are in turn linked to customers who, ultimately, influence the financial perspective of the company (Kaplan & Norton, 1996: 31). By 1996, the Balanced Scorecard was commended as a strategic management tool and, by 2001, it became clear that this cause and effect chain was intended to visualise a generic process for the creation and delivery of value to both customers and shareholders. In 2004, the Balanced Scorecard was described as "...one of the most influential management ideas of the past 15 years" (ICAEW, 2003: 23).

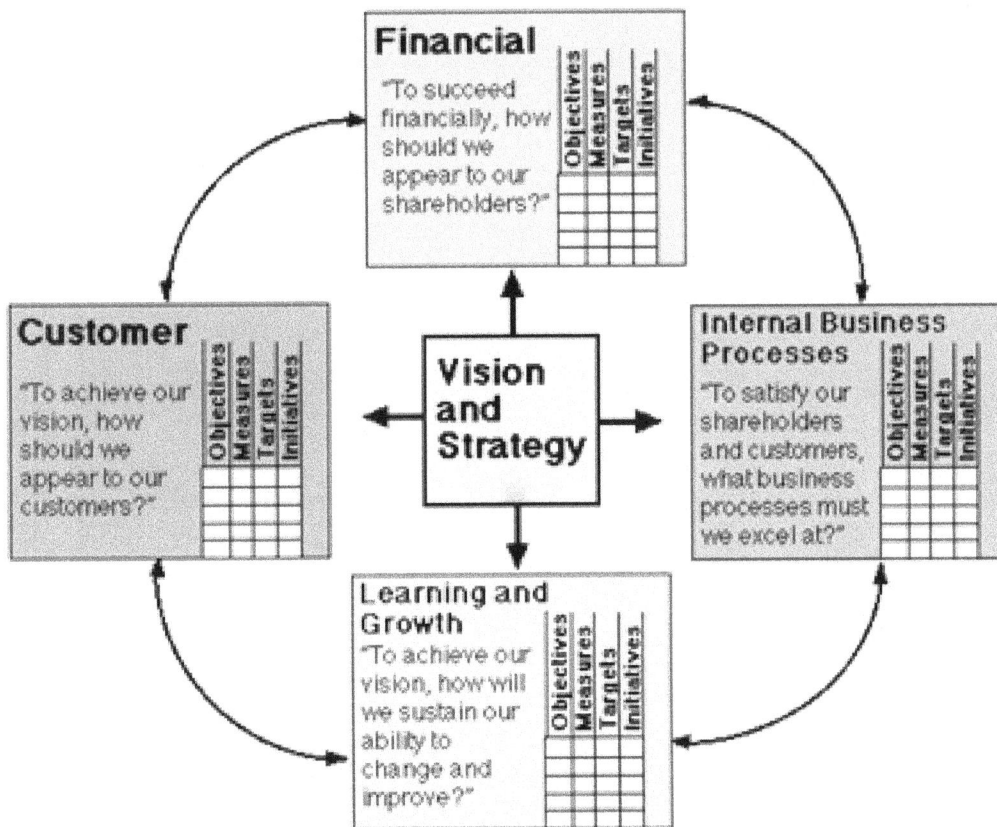

Figure 15: Balanced Scorecard anno 1996 (Kaplan & Norton 1996)

Kaplan & Norton (2001; 2004) use the Balanced Scorecard to develop the Strategy Map which they describe as the game plan of the enterprise and a tool to help management to accomplish long term goals and objectives of the company. Although financial objectives (such as return on capital employed) sit at the head of the Strategy Map, Kaplan and Norton recognise that the key to the success of an enterprise is customer loyalty which is developed through market offerings (value propositions). Kaplan and Norton maintain that, where customer loyalty is secured, financial targets are also likely to be achieved and ultimately shareholders will see their own value creation and delivery expectations fulfilled. In order to meet the expectations of the customer base, it is necessary for the enterprise to ensure that its various internal business processes are effectively configured and operated. Vital to this process is the appropriate utilisation of the resource base of the enterprise, with particular importance being placed on the creation and reproduction of a highly competent and committed workforce.

Financial Perspective

Productivity Strategy · Growth Strategy

Long-Term Shareholder Value

Improve Cost Structure · Increase Asset Utilization · Expand Revenue Opportunities · Enhance Customer Value

Customer Perspective

Customer Value Proposition

Price · Quality · Availability · Selection · Functionality · Service · Partnership · Brand

Product / Service Attributes · Relationship · Image

Internal Perspective

Operations Management Processes	Customer Management Processes	Innovation Processes	Regulatory and Social Processes
• Supply • Production • Distribution • Risk Management	• Selection • Acquisition • Retention • Growth	• Opportunity ID • R&D Portfolio • Design/Develop • Launch	• Environment • Safety and Health • Employment • Community

Learning and Growth Perspective

Human Capital

Information Capital

Organization Capital

Culture · Leadership · Alignment · Teamwork

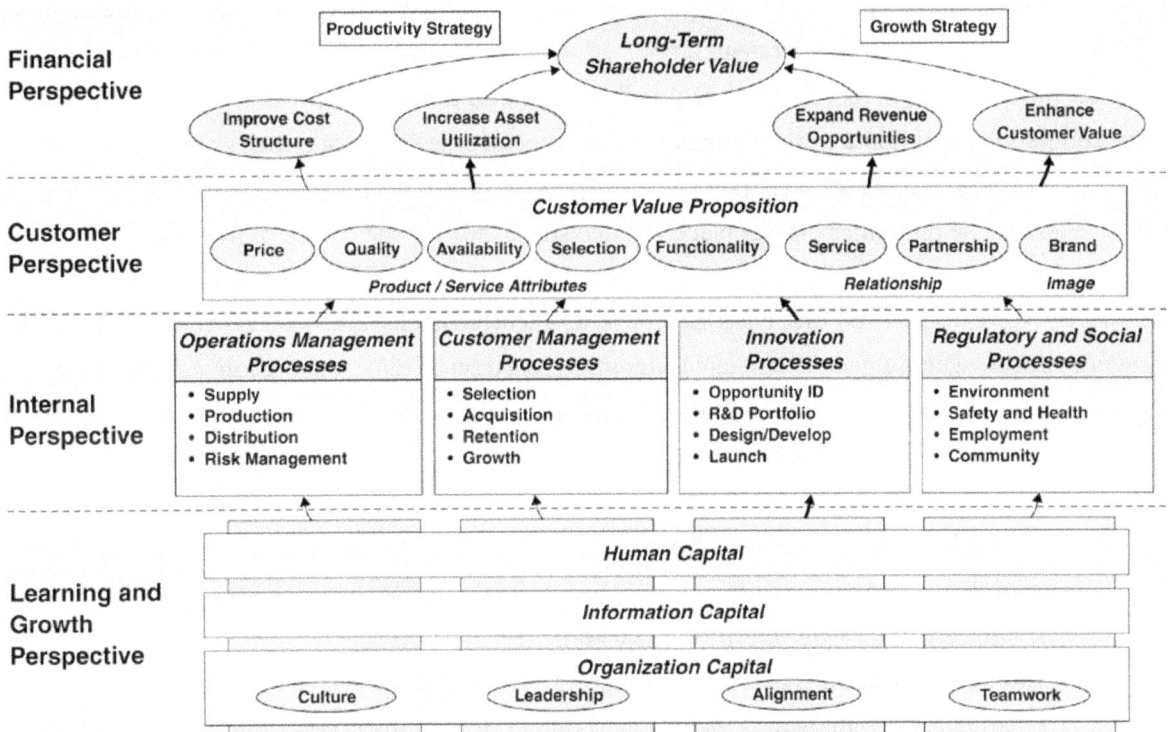

Figure 16: Strategy maps (Kaplan & Norton 2001)

According to Balanced Scorecard the basic theory for the economic company control is that it is based on the strategy of the company. As mentioned above, the financial budget constitutes the future plans of the company, translated into monetary units. If the company should move into a specific direction, such strategic views should be incorporated in the financial budget.

Similarly, if you want to influence actions carried out in the company with regard to implementing the plans of the company, you should also evaluate the steps which bring the company in the desired direction.

You will be able to find a number of other management models, which like the Balanced Scorecard are based on the outlined basic principles, such as: The Business Excellence Model, Total Quality Management, Business Model Analysis and Knowledge Statements.

4.3.1 Strategic understanding

The Balanced Scorecard is an example of how to manage your company by combining non-financial performance goals and financial performance goals. In the beginning of the nineties academic circles had a lively debate precisely on the sufficiency by managing on budget deviations alone. Popular phrases such as "If you can't measure it, you can't manage it" and "What gets measured gets done" were among the views which formed the basis for the debate. In his influential article from 1990 The Performance Measurement Manifesto Eccles argued in favour of companies being managed according to a more balanced set of details. By balanced details Eccles means both financial details and non-financial details, as well as details pointing forward and retrospective details.

The positioning perspective is the starting point for the Balanced Scorecard strategy understanding. The theory is that only a few key strategies, referred to as positions in the market place, are advisable in any given industry. The theory is that it is possible to defend the market position against existing and future competitors and that a unique position in the specific market place ensures the highest possible return. The strategic context is the market place which is characterized by finances and competition. The attractiveness of the particular market place is a decisive factor for the choice of position.

The strategic process forming the basis for the BSC theories is characterized by the fact that it is a deliberate process where a generic strategy is designed based on analytic calculation, and the purpose of which is to position the company in the market place. Thus the specific strategic process in connection with Balanced Scorecard passes four phases:

1. The management specifies the financial aims to be achieved, and the market segments to approach
2. The aims are to be achieved through customer satisfaction
3. Customer satisfaction is achieved through the "right" generic value chain model
4. To maintain the right generic value chain model in the future, goals for learning and growth must be defined.

The strategy contents are about choosing a position in the market. The process controlling persons are the top management having the role as designers of the value chain processes. A positioning approach is therefore a distinct outside-in view where the market conditions decide the strategy and thus the structure, the processes and the resources of the particular organization. The strategy which the management conveys to the organization is thus a report on the future profitability profile and market position of the company. The management is obliged to communicate the replies to the following questions to the rest of the organization: "Where is our future market position?" and "How can we compete?"

4.3.2 Managerial challenges

As described in the above sections the Balanced Scorecard is the strategic management tools to implement the strategy of the company, and the point of departure is that the performance level of the company is controlled by four different perspectives which are assumed to inter-relate in the shape of the causal relations. Therefore it is assumed that these four perspectives are based on the strategy of the company. It is obvious to ask the following questions:

Do causal relations exist?

The chain of causal relations assumed to explain the connection between the competences of the employees, through the business model and the financial result of the company, the BSC model calls a strategy map. However, the question is whether the asserted causal relation between the chosen key indicators and the financial results actually exists in the real world?

Are the casual relations linear?

A correct identification of the correlations is vital for the identification of the correct actions. As an example, the correlations between an increased customer satisfaction and customer profitability are hardly linear. Undoubtedly it might be more profitable to use resources on changing a customer satisfied on the average into an extremely satisfied customer than using the resources on the customers who are already extremely satisfied. Thus the correlation is decreasing. Due to the underlying theory that BSC helps to create focus on the right performance measuring seen in relation to the perspective of the company, it would be obvious to ask as follows:

What happens to elements which are not measured?

"What gets measured gets done" is a widespread quote in the management discussions. This is obvious, also seen in the light that many companies connect rewarding systems to achieved results. However, if management focus points only in one direction it goes without saying that other elements will be given a low priority, which might have serious consequences. Therefore it is important constantly to consider whether the measured elements bring the company closer to the actual goal.

4.3.3 Strategy maps

The strategy map process is based on the overall goals and ideologies, and it aims at operationalizing the ambitious ideas and making them tangible, and thereby manageable. Therefore the process starts by looking at the vision and mission of the company to form the basis for the strategy map:

1. Define the vision of the company (what will we be/ achieve?)
2. Evaluate the mission of the company (why are we here?) and account for the core values (what do we believe in?)
3. Work out the strategy of the company (how can we fulfill the vision?)

In this way the company can describe, translate and implement the strategy by means of the strategy map in order to identify the measuring of the achievements related to value creation, financial result and management of the company by means of Balanced Scorecard. In the below subsection the strategy mapping is briefly described with regard to the four perspectives in Balanced Scorecard, i.e. the financial perspective, the customer perspective, the internal perspective and the learning and growth perspective.

Thus, the Strategy Map can provide a wide range of information on the implementation of a company's chosen business model. Precisely how much information is provided depends on a number of factors; for example, only information that is relevant to understanding company performance should be reported. It is not intended that the Strategy Map supersedes the existing financial statements, instead it should provide supplementary information that helps stakeholders understand company performance more fully. Likewise, the Strategy Map is not intended to reveal an enterprise's most vital commercial secrets.

4.4　Intellectual capital statements

Intellectual capital reporting was developed to respond to criticisms of a mismatch between the market value of companies and their financial statements. While some contributors sought to put financial values on intangible assets, others pursued a scorecard/index-based approach to intellectual capital values, of which there are now several alternatives: The Skandia Navigator (Edvinsson, 1997), the Intangible Assets Monitor (Sveiby, 1997) and the Value Chain Scoreboard (Lev, 2001). All three of these reporting frameworks exhibit a number of similarities with the Balanced Scorecard and seek to provide a set of relevant indicators of intellectual capital growth using a combination of financial and non-financial information.

Danish researchers are credited with the initial (DATI, 1999, 2001; Mouritsen *et al.* 2003) and subsequent development (The Meritum Report 2002; Bukh and Johanson, 2003) of the Intellectual Capital Statement (ICS). More recently, principles for the production of ICSs have been proposed in Australia (Boedker, 2005). The main difference between the ICS and the scorecard approach to capital reporting is that the former is based in narrative rather than numerical indicators; advocates of the ICS commend the incorporation of a wide range of qualitative reporting, and often talk in terms of visualising intellectual capital rather reporting on it (Fincham and Roslender 2003). Equally, there is always a place for relevant indicators, confirming the view that the ICS is underpinned by an extensive interpretation of what accounting entails (Mouritsen and Larsen 2005).

Its supporters argue that an ICS should communicate a narrative of knowledge resources in a company, the challenges that management face in the process of value creation, the initiatives identified by the company to do so and the resulting performance indicators (Mouritsen *et al.* 2003). The structure of this model is presented in figure 17 below.

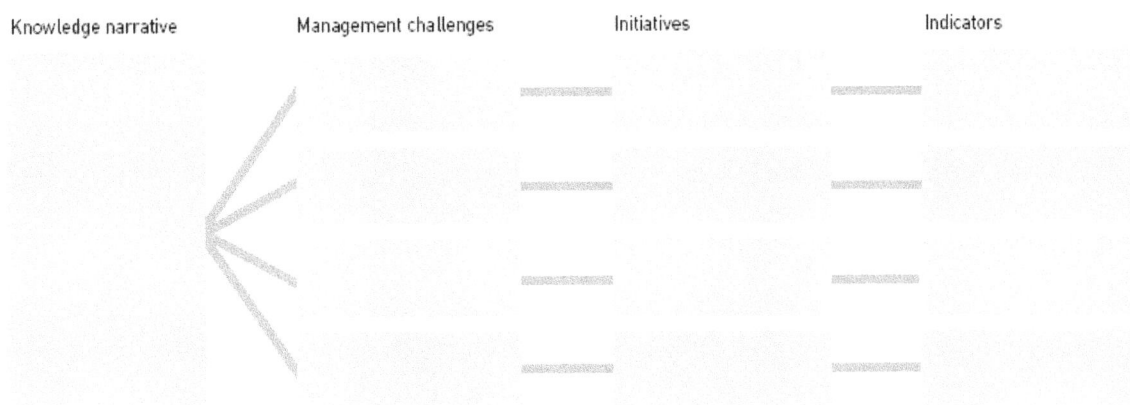

Figure 17: The Danish guideline for intellectual capital statements model (Mouritsen *et al.* 2003: 13)

The knowledge narrative is a story about how the company seeks to create value for its customers through the utilisation of its knowledge resources; it identifies the ambition of the company knowledge management and formulates a strategy for the company know-how in the future. Thus, the knowledge narrative has three elements: (i) how the customer is taken into account by the products or services of the company (the use value); (ii) which knowledge resources (for example, employees, customers, processes and technologies) it must possess to deliver the described use value; and (iii) the particular nature of the product or service in question.

To formulate the knowledge narrative, companies need to provide answers to a number of key questions including: what product or service the company provides; what makes a difference for the customer; what knowledge resources are necessary to be able to supply the product or service; and what is the relationship between value and knowledge resources? The company management challenges are informed by its knowledge narrative and relate to obstacles that the company must overcome to fulfil the ambition that has been set for it. This consideration is also informed by the answers to certain questions including: what are the challenges that the organisation is experiencing; which of the existing knowledge resources of the organization should be strengthened; and what new knowledge resources are required? Together, the knowledge narrative and management challenges contribute to a coherent strategy of knowledge management which results in the identification of a series of initiatives; for example, knowledge containers (such as employees, customers, processes or technologies). Management are required to choose and prioritise these initiatives.

Thus, although the first three elements of an ICS assume a narrative form, they can be supplemented by qualitative information where appropriate (such as illustrations). In the final element, the results of the initiatives are monitored using quantitative indicators, as in scorecard approaches. As ever, the choice of indicators is informed by the information needs believed to be most relevant to users. Already, a number of key indicators have been identified including: staff turnover; job satisfaction; in-service training; turnover analysed by customer; customer satisfaction; precision of supply etc..

Barth *et al.* (2001) argue that traditional financial statements do not represent knowledge resources very well and consequently the Danish initiative was keen to promote ICS as an external reporting mechanism. The audit profession was also encouraged to provide a range of insights on how to make such a reporting framework more credible for external reporting purposes. Experiences from Danish firms issuing ICS (cf. Bukh *et al.* 2001; Mouritsen *et al.* 2001a, 2001b, 2001c, 2002) show that, intellectual capital is not only about knowledge resources in the form of human capital, customer capital, structural capital but also about their complementary attributes; for example, the productivity of one resource may improve by investments in another. It may be that investments in employee development will improve the effectiveness of IT technology, or customer-relations. If this is the case, human capital cannot be separated from organizational capital, or customer capital, and neither is there a causal relationship between them; the overall effectiveness is a collective effect that cannot be explained by the sum of its parts.

Hence, ICSs are not to be read simply by analyzing the indicators and imposing an explanatory model to link the elements in a causal relationship (Mouritsen *et al.* 2001c), instead, ICSs comprise of textual representations, pictures and other indicators about the knowledge management activities of the firm. Consequently, there is no specific ways of reading and interpreting IC reports and this makes the comparison of different IC reports very difficult.

4.5 Chesbroughs open business model framework

Chesbrough & Rosenbloom (2002, 5), define the business model as a construct that integrates previous perspectives on business design into a coherent framework that takes technological characteristics and potentials as inputs, and converts them through customers and markets into economic outputs.

The business model is thus conceived as a focusing device that mediates between technology development and economic value creation. They argue that firms need to understand the cognitive role of the business model, in order to commercialize technology in ways that will allow firms to capture value from their technology investments. Chesbrough & Rosenbloom (2002) identify six elements that make up a business model:

1. Articulate the value proposition, that is, the value created for users by the offering based on the technology
2. Identify a market segment, that is, the users to whom the technology is useful and for what purpose

3. Define the structure of the value chain within the firm required to create and distribute the offering

4. Estimate the cost structure and profit potential of producing the offering, given the value proposition and value chain structure chosen

5. Describe the position of the firm within the value network linking suppliers and customers, including identification of potential complementors and competitors

6. Formulate the competitive strategy by which the innovating firm will gain and hold advantage over rivals

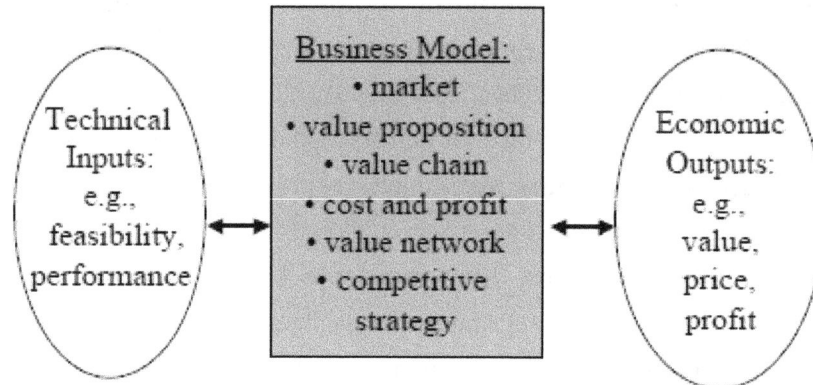

Figure 18: The business model mediates between the technical and economic domains (Chesbrough & Rosenbloom 2002)

In his 2006 book Henry Chesbrough corners the term "Open Business Model" which has many similarities to what we call network-based business models in this book (see chapter 5). An open business model uses both internal and external sources to create value and also uses both internal and external sources to capture a piece of that value. Chesbrough argues that having a better business model is much more worth than merely sitting on a better technology. Further enhancing the competitiveness of business models is that they seem harder to imitate. Chesbrough identifies six stages of business model maturity, which are described below.

Stage 1) Undifferentiated business model

The company with an undifferentiated business model is characterized as selling commodities, not being able to differentiate itself, be driven forth by hard work, hustle, and luck. Such companies have difficulties in attracting capital and they are not scalable. Good examples of this according to Chesbrough are most restaurants.

Stage 2) Differentiated business model

The company with a differentiated business model has a performance advantage, but is characterized by being driven forth by ad hoc processes. Thus it is hard to sustain in the long term. Most differentiated businesses are in the words of Chesbrough "one hit wonders", e.g. most technology startups.

Stage 3) Segmented business model

A company utilizing a segmented business model is able to serve multiple segments, thus generating more profits via a greater volume and lower relative capacity costs. This business model is more sustainable, still it is too internally focused to hit the freeway according to Chesbrough. Good examples of such companies are most industrial firms including one of Chesbrough's favorite examples, Xerox.

Stage4) Externally aware business model

The externally aware business model is able to harness external sources of technology to complement those present internally. This gives a greater momentum for the same invested capital as well as the ability to share risks and rewards. This model broadens the potential market to serve, and good examples are the ERP system provider SAP R/3 and most Big Pharma companies.

Stage 5) Integrated business model

In integrated business models, external sources are routinely utilized to fuel the existing business model. Furthermore, unused internal ideas are allowed to flow outside to the business models of other companies, hence the company becomes a systems integrator of internal and external technologies. Examples of such business are Nike and Procter & Gamble.

Stage 6) Platform leadership business model

At the ultimate stage, the platform leadership business model stage, the company now benefits from investments of others in the platform. The company can induce investment through its suppliers, customers, and other third parties. In this ideal stage a complete business ecosystem is created. Here the company must balance value creation with value capture, and be careful that it does not become predatory, as this would destroy the ecosystem. Examples of such companies are Apple, .NET, WebSphere, Dell, and WalMart.

4.6　Business model canvas

Another more recent contribution to the field of business model conceptualization is Osterwalder *et al.*'s Business Model Canvas (2010). Here the value proposition links the infrastructure of the company (down-stream activities and management to execution) with the customer (distribution and after sales relationships). In comparison to Bell *et al.* (1997), Osterwalder *et al.* (2010) get somewhat closer to the goal of identifying the 'how' of the business model because they place the value proposition at the centre of the model as an aligning feature between infrastructure interrelations such as competences, partner network and value configuration, and customer interrelations such as customer relationships, distribution channel, and target customers.

Business Model Canvas

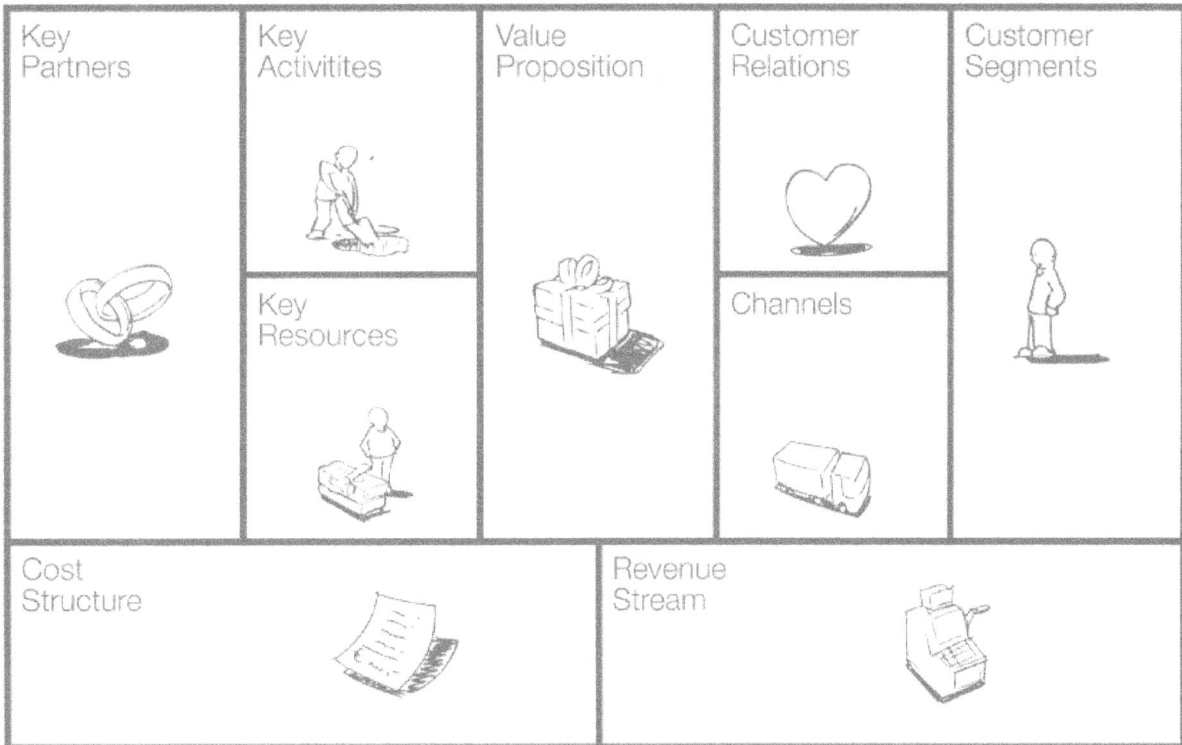

Figure 19: Business Model Canvas (Osterwalder *et al.* 2010)

The Business Model Canvas is a template from which to discuss the "how's" and "why's" of the activities and choices made by a company in order to achieve a sustainable position in their industry. The model does not prescribe any particular starting point for the analysis, or any particular order of discussion. Rather, it prompts the user(s) to focus on natural connectivities between the nine building blocks that make up the model. Osterwalder *et al.* (2010) propose a process of applying the canvas to describe the "as-is" model of the organization, and thereafter to focus on strengths and weaknesses and finally try to narrow down potential "could-be's" and evaluating this business model innovation in a SWOT-like manner. The outcome of the business modeling process is a clearer understanding of the uniqueness of the company and how it addresses the needs of its target customers.

Sum-up questions for chapter 4

- Compare the underlying theoretical backgrounds of the 6 models presented
- Discuss how the Service-Profit Chain addresses the value proposition of a company
- Relate the process perspective of the Strategic Systems Auditing framework to the process perspective of the Strategy Map
- What are the complementarities between Strategy Maps and Intellectual Capital Statements?
- Discuss how Chesbrough's framework for Open Business Models can be related to the Business Model Canvas

5 Network-based business models

For several decades the success and ultimately also the sustainability of businesses has been problematized in the light of societal and industrial developments. Among other issues the rise of the importance of intangibles and sustainability issues has put pressures on the profitability of businesses, as well as the actions of policy-makers and professional bodies alike. Numerous examples of how new business values are gaining momentum in relation to the value proposition of organizations surface, pressuring organizations to surrender profits for ethical reasons, and in this sense how the market may endure greater power than policy-makers. We need to start accounting for value creating; not value creation.

As such, the rise of new business models, e.g. based on loosely coupled networks and multisided platforms of value creation, potentially pose a large threat to the stability and structure of organization and value-realization as we know it. Perhaps it can even be argued that e.g. accounting and jurisdiction as we know it, will become obsolete in a world of network organizations and social-community based business models, thus posing new conceptions of accountability and creating new sets of stakeholder tensions.

Despite such developments in business, i.e. communities, knowledge, collaboration, networks, innovation, professions such as accounting, finance and law have not kept pace. Not to mention policy-making. Thus from a management perspective we may need to ask: "How do we produce decision-relevant information?" and "How do we capture value creation and value realizing transactions?" Furthermore, we may need to ask: "How do we validate information across structures that do not exist per se"? Finally, implications for policy-making and accounting bodies need to be evaluated.

The ventures of the network economy are different than those of past decades. Hence, we need to go beyond business combination-based joint venture thinking and even beyond network-accounting. Here we are concerned with virtual companies constituted by mutually beneficial business partners. Here notions of virtual value and connectivity capital become cornerstones of understanding value creation.

In this book we describe different views on business models, how to understand them, analyze and describe them. We can either focus on business models as the business model for the company or as individual elements of it, but this is limited to the company focus, e.g. as is evident in the Osterwalder business model canvas he includes partners complimenting the key activity and resources that are in the company, allowing business modelling to include partners – but partners can be an inevitable part of a business model – In this chapter we introduce examples of different types of network-based business models.

5.1   What defines a network based business model?

A network based business model is a model including two or several stakeholders creating a joint value proposition based on the stakeholders key activities and resources. This can be done as open business models or Business Network Business Models (BNBM) where local or even global network partners gain significant competitive advantage and growth through creating network based business models. Companies will in future need to understand that they have entered a new era – one that is based on new principles, worldviews – new business network business models – where the business model playing rules are significantly changed compared to what we have known until today.

We already know that collective knowledge; in some instances called "intellectual capital" or knowledge resources put into broad horizontal networks of participants can be mobilized to create far more value than a single company can do alone.

The financial crises showed that companies cut their cost to a minimum reducing key resources and activities in their business model, some resulting in limiting the value proposition to customer – It is almost inherent that when a company needs to cut costs, e.g. Scandinavian Airlines, it will have an impact on the service provided to the customers. Evidence suggests that new business models in the future be based on openness, peering, sharing, and global positioning, will enable the possibility to reduce cost by partnering instead of thinking the business model as a single levelled model.

The speed with which changes and the ever increasing demand for new business models and processes are challenging companies, many are well aware that they can no longer rely on their own internal capabilities and competencies to survive. Nor can they rely on tight, rigid and inflexible relationships with only a few business partners – for a keep pace with customers' increasing desire for speed, innovation and control. Companies must in the future engage, and build a development area with many people – partners, competitors, stakeholders, and not least – customers. "Mass Collaboration" is a necessary part of any company's innovation strategy.

A company's ability to connect and disconnect to these networks, business models and processes and its ability to innovate across the network capabilities represent themselves to be one – must.

5.2 Barriers and challenges

The development of new interdisciplinary network, however, contains a number of new barriers and challenges for both businesses and researchers. Although it will be the central hub for innovation and development of global business models, they are very few companies "leveraged" to practice the innovation of business models in the network. It goes without saying that companies are "handicapped" by their creation of a corporate culture and learning culture which was characterized by hierarchy, "single business model thinking," Planning and push and pull economy.

It requires an entirely new knowledge, research and new businesses to cope with "mass collaboration" and "multi-business model" (Lindgren, Taran and Boer 2009) economy. However, it is not enough to be able to get the ideas and concepts for new business models "merged" together – but it is also necessary to act on them commercialize them quickly, globally – and thus to different markets.

This must necessarily on the research side be based on a structured innovation research strategy developed in close collaboration with researchers from all interested innovation communities, companies and knowledge competencies (GTS, Knowledge Consultants, etc.) as well as professional development and service operators who have an interest in developing the area.

Sum-up questions for chapter 5

- Why have network-based business models gained so much momentum in recent years?
- Define a network-based business model
- Give your own example of a network-based business model

6 Value creation maps

The problem – as well as the prospect – with business models is that they are concerned with being different; the business needs a unique selling point. So the bundle of indicators on strategy, intellectual capital, and so on that will be relevant to analysis or disclosure will differ from firm to firm. The information needs to be communicated – in the strategic context of the firm, as this would show its relevance to the value creation process in the company. It does not make sense to insert such information into a standardized accounting regime. We would point out that if it is difficult for the company itself to conceptualize the business model, then it will probably be even more difficult for external parties to analyze it. At present there exists very little literature on the different aspects of analyzing business models.

When we perceive relationships and linkages, they more often than not reflect some kind of tangible transactions, i.e. the flow of products, services or money. When perceiving and analyzing the value transactions going on inside an organization, or between an organization and its partners, there is a marked tendency to neglect or forget the often parallel intangible transactions and interrelations that are also involved.

So, to create a more meaningful analysis and understanding of a business model, we need to assemble a new cocktail of tools including, as essential ingredients, intangible transactions and relationships. Although our work has so far been primarily focused on network-based business models, the conclusions seem easily generalizable to other settings.

We have found it useful to integrate the generic tangible and intangible transactions from the value network mapping perspective of Verna Allee (2011) with the notions of cognitive maps, and finally to place these aspects in the strategic notions of the Intellectual Capital Guideline (Mouritsen *et al.* 2003a) and the Analytical Model (Mouritsen *et al.* 2003b). In union, these ideas materialize into the value creation map!

6.1   What is the value creation process?

Value creation is now the main aim of any company. Creating value means to generate economic wealth, that is, to obtain a performance improvement in terms of increased sales or decreased costs. The value creation process depends on the combination of value drivers considered important by the company. A value driver can take two forms. It can be a tangible resource (e.g. machinery) or an intangible resource (e.g. trademarks, employees' competences) available to the company. It can also be a critical success factor considered important by customers and that the company can influence (e.g. product quality, customer satisfaction, product innovation). It is this specific combination of resources and critical success factors that leads to the generation of value. However, companies do not create value in the same fashion. Different companies create value in different ways.

This process, in fact, is strongly firm-specific as it is intrinsically linked to the features of the company in which it takes place. It strictly depends on the contingent factors that affect the business context: the vision, the mission, the strategic priorities, the relationships between managers and employees as well as all those factors that make the way in which the company operates unique and unrepeatable. For example, the managers' knowledge about the competitive dynamics of a particular sector can contribute to the creation of value only if the company plans to compete in that sector.

Since the 1980's, increased competition and the advent of information and communication technologies have turned the value creation process of companies into something that has become more and more dynamic and complex. In fact, value creation does not depend only on individual value drivers, but rather, on the relationships among them. Therefore, the value drivers are not rigidly separated and each of them does not develop in its own way, independently of the others, following its own logic. It is impossible to identify *a priori* the features and functions of the resources in a company because they depend on the original combination that is set up in the specific company context. Moreover, the relationships among the value drivers are not stable; they do not always display the same features and they may even cease to exist or change intensity, direction and nature.

Managers' actions that are expected to affect a specific business asset may, however, also be relevant to other resources. This is the reason why the relationships among value drivers are often fragile, ambiguous and potential. Relationships among the resources of a company can be non-linear: this is the case when key employees decide to switch to the competitors, for example. This change can destabilize the entire business system with negative impacts on the value creation process. For these reasons, it is becoming more and more important for companies to be able to manage the value creation process. This is possible through the visualization of the value drivers involved in the value creation process and, above all, through the representation of the relationship network that links resources and critical success factors and leads to value creation. The awareness of the causal relationships, of their strength and of their nature allows the company to effectively and efficiently manage the value drivers. In this way, in fact, companies can take appropriate decisions in order to influence the situation in the desired direction and to increase the creation of value.

6.2   Why might the value creation process be difficult to discover?

Managing the value creation process can be a very difficult task. The knowledge of the value drivers involved, of the way in which they combine with each other, of the nature and the intensity of the relationships are rarely formalized and shared in the company. This knowledge, in fact, belongs to the managers who work within the company. They manage, on a daily basis, the value drivers and the causal links in order to increase the value created for the company. Their awareness of the contribution that each value driver provides to the value creation process drives their actions and their decisions.

For example, a manager may find a strong and positive relationship between the value driver "employee competences" and the value driver "product quality". This belief is going to lead the manager to make decisions in order to:

1. Raise the skills level of employees through training, for example
2. Encourage employees to provide as many suggestions as possible

If the manager's perception is correct, these two types of actions should have a positive effect on the product quality and, consequently, on the creation of value.

However, the knowledge of the value drivers and their relationships is tacit and therefore, difficult to access and to visualize. Managers themselves find this kind of knowledge hard to elicit and to manage. Even when an analysis is made through written reports, these do not always contain a clear description of the assumptions made on the dynamic relationships among the value drivers that underpin the creation of value. This is because the need to rapidly solve the day-to-day problems leaves little room for conceptualization and reflective activities.

In this perspective, managers are considered to be information workers because they spend a lot of their time absorbing and processing information on problems and opportunities. One of the fundamental challenges that managers face is that their environments are extremely complex, from an information point of view. In order to understand managers' actions, it is necessary to build and analyze the content (value drivers) and structure (relationships among value drivers) of the mental models through which they filter information, structure knowledge and make decisions. Therefore, it is necessary to use a tool which can facilitate this operation, by making explicit managers' knowledge of the way in which the company generates value.

6.3   What is a value creation map?

A value creation map is a tool that makes it possible to visualize and to explain the managers' mental models, reproducing the specific ways in which a company creates value. A value creation map is made up of two elements: nodes and arrows. The nodes of the map are the value drivers which the management considers important to value creation. The arrows, instead, identify the relationships among the value drivers. The thickness of the arrow indicates the strength of the relationship. The relationships among the value drivers can be of different natures:

1. Positive, when one value driver positively affects another one. In this case, the arrow is matched with a plus sign
2. Negative, when one value driver negatively affects another one. In this case, the arrow is matched with a minus sign
3. Doubtful, when the influence of one value driver on another one is uncertain.

The value creation map enables us to understand the ways in which managers perceive the succession of events, give meaning to the relationships between the events themselves and evaluate alternative courses of action.

As with the use of geographical maps, with value creation maps, too, we can assume that a certain "path", made up of decisions and actions, is going to lead to a particular "destination", that is, the creation of value. This tool makes it possible to identify the most important value drivers and to visualize the relationship network among them, representing the peculiar way in which value is generated in a given company context.

6.4 The building process: A two-step method

The building process of a value creation map aims to elicit the mental models that are triggered in managers, in certain situations. As mentioned before, these models have a largely tacit nature because they are deeply embedded in individuals and they are rarely made explicit. This conversion is a very hard task because the value drivers and the relationships among them are difficult to explain and communicate so that managers themselves consider the interpretation of the decision rules that drive their actions very critical.

The building process of a value creation map consists of two steps: firstly, the elicitation of the value drivers considered important by the managers and secondly, the identification of relationships among the value drivers. Before analyzing each step, it is relevant to clarify what kind of managers and how many managers should be involved in the building process of the value creation map.

6.4.1 What kind of managers? How many managers?

A critical aspect, already in the design stage of the map, relates to the identification of what kind of managers and how many managers should be involved in the development of the value creation map. Obviously, these choices are linked to the size and the features of the company to be analyzed, so the following should be considered general considerations.

Unanimous opinions in the field argue that the identification of the value drivers and the relationships among them is up to the top managers, because they are the ones who are going to use the map and they have the skills needed to support its building. However, a purely strategic vision does not seem enough when the aim is to identify the links between individual actions and effects. The operative knowledge possessed by middle management helps to better identify the nature and intensity of the relationships and to consider the potential impact of the value drivers that top managers may not be able to assess. Therefore, before proceeding to the map building, it is particularly important to identify the management levels to be involved, according to their skills and their expertise.

Concerning the number of managers to involve, previous studies on value mapping show that involving three to five individuals is sufficient to obtain adequate knowledge of the value creation process and avoids making the map building process too complex.

6.4.2 First step: Identifying the value drivers

The aim of the first step is to identify the value drivers considered relevant by the managers for the purpose of creating value. The tools that appear to be the most suitable for this purpose are the semi-structured and the unstructured interview. The questionnaire and the structured interview, instead, are not very flexible or adaptable to specific situations and this makes them inappropriate for explaining the contents of the mental model created by a manager in a given situation. Both the semi-structured interview as well as the unstructured one, in contrast, has an high degree of flexibility. They allow deep access to the conceptual categories used by the manager, by identifying his/her interpretations of reality and the motivations that drive his/her decisions.

These interviews should be conducted at the individual level as tacit knowledge is personal and not always shared within a team of managers, even though they may work closely together for a long time. Interviewing managers allows them to reflect on the actions that they usually put in place. In this way, the researcher can discover aspects of behavior which were tacit until that moment. The first question to ask should be a general one, such as: "What are the factors that lead to the success of the company?". The aim is to gradually uncover deeper and deeper layers of the managers' knowledge. In order to identify the causes that affect the value drivers, it is important to ask managers to tell anecdotes and give examples, some positive and others negative, regarding factors that have generated success or failure in the company. Asking them for anecdotes and examples is particularly powerful because it forces managers to explain what really happens, it stimulates them to provide details and triggers, in turn, other thoughts and stories. Through story and language, in fact, managers give meaning to events that occur and to their actions and they can organize their experience. In this way, it is possible to discover how the value drivers come "into action" in the company under analysis. After finishing the interviews, the researcher analyzes the transcripts in order to prepare a list containing the value drivers considered critical by the managers interviewed.

6.4.3 Second step: Identifying the relationships among value drivers

The second step aims to identify the causal relationships among the value drivers in the list. In particular, there are two methods that can be employed for this purpose. In the first method, the researcher interprets and identifies the relationships among the value drivers in the list. In particular, he/she is responsible for identifying the strength and the direction of causal links through his/her understanding of the company context (resulting from past and present experience) and the interpretation of the managers' perceptions. The second method, however, requires the managers previously interviewed to identify the relationships among the value drivers in the list. This can be done through the creation of a focus group. This second option is preferable for several reasons.

Through interaction and discussion, the members of the focus group can reflect on their behaviors and on those of others, bringing into question the meaning of the value drivers and the relationships that are activated in specific situations. At this stage, managers are also called upon to express their opinion on the intensity and the sign of the relationships, while the researcher has to provide them with the greatest possible support, but should avoid leading them to pre-determined results.

The meaning of the value drivers comes from language. In particular, the meanings are developed and refined during the interaction and discussion in the focus groups: the meaning of the value drivers becomes clear to a manager from the reactions that their use provokes in other managers. Therefore, the value drivers and the relationships among them which are contained in a value creation map are formed through interaction and discussion.

Managers are encouraged by the researcher to modify and enrich the map, by adding, removing or moving value drivers and relationships. This process allows them, on the one hand, to analyze the evolution process of the map and, on the other hand, to understand the perspectives of others.

The above mentioned process leads to a map which is "owned" by the focus group members. It allows them to achieve a deeper sharing of the meanings given to the previously identified value drivers in the list. Furthermore, during this step, the creativity of managers is greatly stimulated, so new value drivers, not originally identified in the list, may emerge from the group discussion.One of the main challenges in the building process of value creation maps concerns the study of social processes that enable the group to acquire and shape information and to make shared decisions. Regardless of the method chosen to identify the relationships among the value drivers, the aim of the building process is to create a map similar to that represented below.

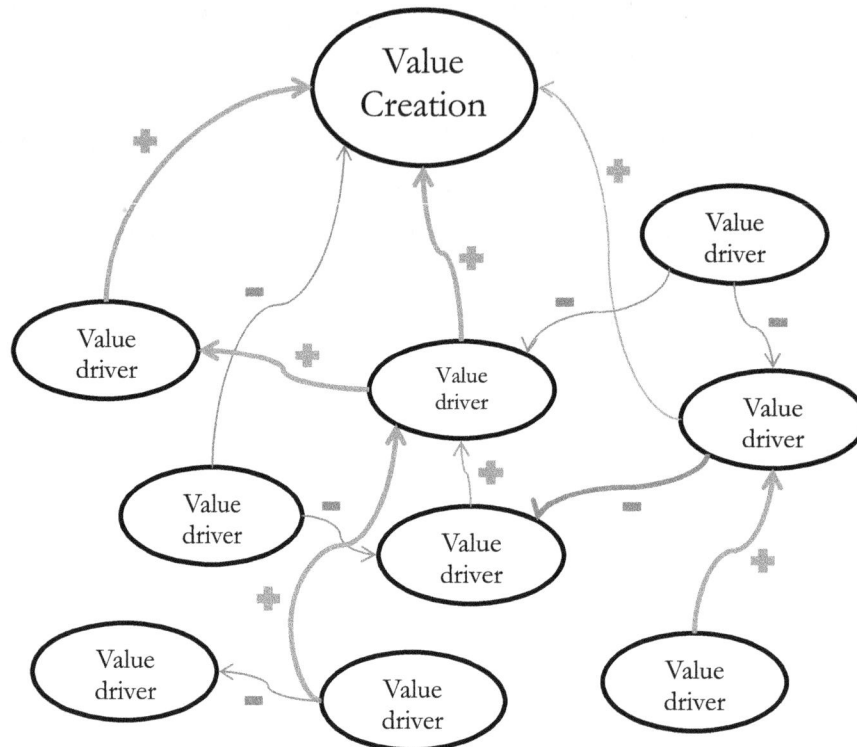

Figure 20: The value creation map

6.5 Refining the value creation map

As it should be clear from the previous paragraph, the value creation map created at the end of the building process cannot be considered definitive. The intrinsic instability of the value drivers, but above all of the relationships identified, determines the need for updating and refining the map previously developed. This need can be felt as a result of a change in the conditions inside or outside the company. This can affect the relationships identified before or can create new links. The awareness of these changes, in fact, alters the managers' perceptions and assumptions which led to the building of the "initial" value creation map.

Furthermore, the need to update the map can emerge from the actual deployment of business processes. This can reveal the real effects of managerial actions on the value drivers and the value creation process. So, it is only natural that there can be differences between the "initial" map, developed on the basis of the assumptions expressed by managers, and "in progress" maps, progressively updated in order to take into due consideration the changing internal and external conditions.

Even when an "initial" map is substantially different from the "updated" maps, the tool does not lose its effectiveness. The value creation map, in fact, is dynamic in nature. The differences should serve as a boost for managers to reflect on what relationships have actually occurred, to understand the reasons why the "initial" relationships have not taken place and, therefore, to understand how to set them up again. Thus, the instability of the content of the value creation map is a "technical" feature that enhances the role of this tool in supporting management's learning process.

6.6 Value creation maps and indicators

The building of the value creation map can be considered the basis for setting up a measurement system. In particular, the map can be considered the skeleton on which to build an appropriate set of indicators (I). These indicators should be coupled to the nodes of the map.

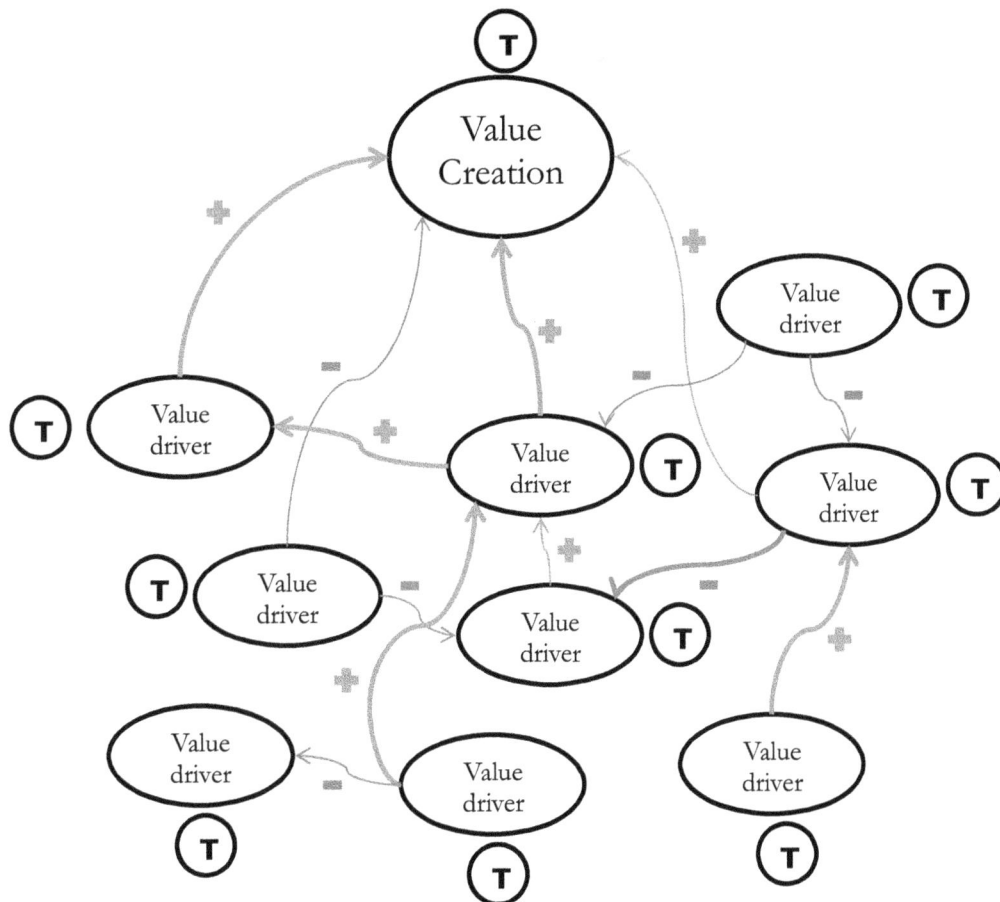

Figure 21: The value creation map with indicators

The use of a value creation map as the foundation upon which to build a specific set of indicators can improve the selectiveness of the measurement system. The focus on critical aspects of the value creation process avoids the risk of squandering management's attention by providing an excessive number of indicators. Moreover, a measurement system built on the basis of a value creation map allows an appropriate balance between lagging indicators, mainly financial, and leading indicators, typically quantitative-physical and qualitative. This is because the development of a value creation map makes it possible to identify the drivers of the value creation and to trace the causes that affect it.

The conciseness, accuracy and reliability of lagging indicators is useful for nodes downstream of the value creation map, that is, those associated with the value drivers directly linked to the value creation. These indicators are not so difficult to design and to build, but they are oriented to the past, so they do not have the ability to reflect the current activities. The inclusion of leading indicators, built on a specific node and a specific relationship, are able to provide prompt signals and to monitor and govern the deep causes of value creation. In this way, these indicators can anticipate the final results and drive the performance of lagging measures.

Furthermore, the correspondence between the value creation map and indicators provides the management with relevant information on the timing of actions on the value drivers. In particular, monitoring the trend of indicators over time can help to "capture" the length of the lag, i.e. the time it takes for an indicator of a value driver to begin to influence the indicators of related value drivers, first, and influence the financial performance, later. For example, a measure that "captures" the effectiveness of research and development activities (e.g. number of patents) is not likely to affect the financial performance in the short-term.

It probably needs a temporal lag of several years. In contrast, leading indicators related to product quality (e.g.: defect rates and on-time deliveries) can influence the economic and financial indicators with a shorter lag. Managers should pay attention to this aspect because the lack of an immediate effect on financial performance may simply mean that actions take time before generating an economic benefit. Therefore, management actions that may be deleted or changed because they generate no immediate effects, might instead be "reconsidered" when managers become aware of their potential effects in the medium and long term.

The "matching" between value creation and map indicators, moreover, can provide useful information on the persistence of the effect of a particular action on value drivers, i.e. how long the effect persists once it is started. In fact, the effect may be only temporary and affect the indicator trend of the value driver to which the action is directed only for a short period of time. Or, the effect may persist and influence the indicator trend for longer periods of time.

Finally, indicators can play a leading role in the refining and updating process of the map. The relationships among the value drivers are, by their nature, unstable. In this sense, the dynamics of the indicator is of primary importance in order to test the existence of the relationship and to verify its trend over time, since the intensity of the links may not be unvaried. In other words, indicators may signal effects on the value drivers that are not manifesting themselves with the timing or the intensity which had been considered in the "initial" map. This can provide useful information on possible changes to be made in order to refine and update the map over time. This gives the system a high degree of flexibility and adaptability which is consistent with the dynamics of the value creation process.

6.7. Pros and cons

The building and the use of a value creation map can be very useful for managers. The advantages are mainly related to the effects that this tool can have on their management and learning skills. The visualization of the value drivers and the relationships among them allows managers to understand the strengths and weaknesses of the value creation process. This provides them with the opportunity to maximize the former and lessen the latter, through a more aware management of the individual value drivers and the relationships among them. In this way managers can make the value creation process in the company less fragile and vulnerable because they can avoid the risk that some value drivers remain unmanaged.

Managers' awareness of the creation of value increases not only during the map building process, but especially during the refining and updating process. It must be highlighted that the most important benefit of this stage, in fact, consists in management learning: the refinement of the managers' perceptions and assumptions improves their ability to interpret and manage the dynamics of value drivers and the direct and indirect effects of same on value creation.

The matching between map and indicators further enhances this aspect. Such a measurement system makes it possible to understand the impact of a managerial action on a specific value driver through the analysis of the change of the indicator. From this essentially static perspective, the map allows the switch to a dynamic view by examining, first, the direct impact also on indicators of other related value drivers and, where possible, the indirect impact on value creation. For example, the map could highlight a positive relationship between the value driver "collaboration with employees", matched to the indicator "number of suggestions for each employee", and the value driver "product quality ", associated to the measure" defect rate ".

This matching permits the measurement not only of the individual value drivers, but also of the relationships among them, providing the opportunity to manage that link and to increase the positive impact of a value driver on the related ones. Such a measurement system is strongly oriented to action as it can provide relevant and timely information to support the managers' decision making. The identification of indicators from the mental model of managers who manage the value creation process daily increases the overall quality as well as the signaling ability of the measures system. This can progressively lead to an increased likelihood that decisions cause a series of multiple effects consistent with the expected results.

Therefore, the map represents an important tool to improve decision making when managers are faced with complex and ambiguous situations. The simplified representation of reality perceived by managers can help to identify and to consider alternative courses of action, as well as to choose the option considered appropriate in order to increase the value creation.

However, it must also be noted that there is a drawback linked to the use of value creation maps. It consists in the potential attitudes of resistance or rejection of the tool. The development of value creation map requires, in fact, the willingness to explain and bring into question the interpretative models of managers. This demands a significant time investment in reflection and conceptualization activities. Not all managers may be available or willing to devote time to eliciting their knowledge about the value creation process in the specific company. Therefore, the possibility that the use of value creation maps can generate the effects previously described is also affected by these considerations.

Sum-up questions for chapter 6

- Why might the value creation process be difficult to discover?
- What is a value creation map?
- How can a value creation map be built and refined?
- Why can matching a value creation map to indicators be useful for managers?
- What are the pros and the cons of building and using a value creation map?

7 Business model innovation

Due to today's 'hypercompetition' (D'Aveni 1994) in a globalizing world, companies in all industries worldwide find themselves competing in ever changing environments. Those changes force companies to rethink their operational business models more frequently and more fundamentally, as innovation based solely on new products and aimed towards local markets is no longer sufficient to sustain their competitiveness and survival. Competitors can relatively easily copy products, and local market segments today are often quickly captured by global rivals located elsewhere.

The IBM global CEO study 2006 held among 765 top CEOs is also in favor of that claim – business model innovation matters. Competitive pressures have pushed business model (BM) innovation much higher than expected on industrial priority lists. According to that study, approx. 30 percent of CEOs are pursuing business model innovation initiatives and quite rightly so.

However in most cases, managers' strategic preference typically involves "more of the same" (mostly product) innovations that keep their company fixed on the same line of value propositions, using the same, or somewhat similar, technologies, aimed at the same target customer (e.g. Christensen, 1997). Consequently, the business model in many of those cases is accepted to be fixed on a certain way of doing business, and for that reason it has hardly ever been questioned or changed significantly.

Unfortunately, business models and their innovation are a huge challenge, both theoretically and practically. Much is known about innovation – especially radical product innovation, much less specific business model innovation theory has been developed. And although many managers are very eager to consider more disruptive changes to their business model, they do not usually quite know how to articulate their existing or desired business model, or, even less so, understand the possibilities, or rather the processes, available for innovating it.

The objective of this chapter is therefore to propose several processes that are available for companies for innovating their business models.

7.1   Method

Ten retrospective case studies of BM innovation processes undertaken by two industrial companies (see Table 3) provide the empirical basis for this paper. We selected these companies based on their (relatively) successful, yet somewhat different, BM innovation experiences over the years. The study started early 2009 and is still in progress.

	Company Alpha	Company Beta
Description	Large, global company specialized in developing, manufacturing and marketing (mostly) professional audio products.	Large, global company specialized in developing, manufacturing and marketing flexible electrical/ electronic control and instrumentation solutions within power production, marine and offshore.

Table 3: Case company descriptions and interviews taken

To ensure the validity and reliability of the overall research, multiple qualitative methods were used to collect the data. The data collection was done through desk and field research. The desk research involved collecting of information through books, articles, websites, as well as documents received from the two companies. The field research consisted of face-to-face interviews with managers who had actively participated in, or had been in charge of, the new business development initiative, along with e-mail correspondence, company visits, and questionnaires.

Given the mostly explorative nature of the research we used a semi-structured (standard) questionnaire, which allowed the individual respondents maximum freedom to explain their views on the new business model and their understanding of the innovation process, and enabled us to collect the data we felt we needed for the purpose of our research at the same time. Since the case studies were analyzed retrospectively, the data could not be acquired through observations. Table 4 summarizes the case study data collected.

	Company Alpha	Company Beta
The ten business model innovation cases and their success rates.	• **Case A** – New business unit offering existing and new technology-based products to a new market (automotive) – very successful • **Case B** – New business unit offering existing technology-based products to a new market (mobile phones) – partly successful • **Case C** – New business unit offering existing technology-based products to a new market (studios), plus outsourcing of marketing and sales to a partner – failure • **Case D** – Joint venture, a new technology-based product that can be used in many industries – very successful • **Case E** – Joint venture with a venture fund. The core business is IP and R&D of products based on (mostly) existing technologies for the biomedical industry – very successful • **Case F** – Joint venture offering new technology-based products to a new market (telephone infrastructure), planned to be sold (divested) to a European company – very successful • **Case G** – Outsourcing the manufacturing of one of the products – failure All in all, roughly 60% success in business model innovations.	• **Case 1** – Penetration of the marine industry based on existing and new technological competences. Required internal re-engineering to insure higher quality control and work efficiency (e.g. lean, new business intelligence department) – very successful • **Case 2** – Acquisition of a small company operating in a different industry (wind power). That company currently continues to develop the business internally. Soon to be spun off again as a new independent company – very successful • **Case 3** – New technology-based product, aimed at serving existing and potential new customer segments – failure: after one year of heavy investment in the product, the project was terminated due to incongruity with customer demands (product shape and size; price – too expensive) All in all, roughly 66% success in business model innovations.

Rationality in choice under uncertainty and complexity	**Search processes** – No search process in any of the cases. "*It was just something that came up along the way*". One project was managed proactively in search of a radically new business model (Case F). Otherwise, it was internal competences chosen to be used elsewhere.	**Search processes** – Recognized as one of the weaknesses of the company. They do not really have any systematic processes to manage radical, or even incremental, innovation ideas. It is something that usually just "pops up". They give more attention to ideas that come from their main customers.
	Selection and implementation processes – Following a stage-gate model, radical innovation ideas are handled with extra awareness. A slower process, which always starts with small steps and then grows slowly. Radical ideas follow gates similar to those of incremental ideas. The difference is, though, that it takes more time to move from gate to gate.	**Selection and implementation processes** – A stage-gate model is used to move the business concept idea through a maturity roadmap and development process. Many complaints about the fact that there is not enough market research behind ideas proposed. In effect, lacking understanding of the potential market and sales volume.

Table 4: Summary of the case data

7.2 Analysis

7.2.1 Characteristics of the business model innovation and success rate

Company Alpha: Throughout the years, company Alpha engaged in seven business model innovations. Four cases (A, D, E and F) were very successful. In three cases, the company either partly succeeded (case B), or failed to succeed (cases C and G). All successful cases involved the exploitation of existing technology (case B, C, and E), or the development and exploitation of new technology-based products, together with a partner (cases A, D and F), in a market segment new to company Alpha. Case A resulted in a new internal manufacturing unit; the other success cases in a joint venture. The two failure cases were attempts to outsource the production (case G) or marketing and sales function (case C) to a third party.

Two factors caused their failure. First, the partner did not match the company's high quality standards. Second, they realized in a later phase (particularly case C) that the market was too small to play a significant part in the company's turnover. In case B, company Alpha and a partner company combined some of their competences and developed two mobile phone types. One product was a partial success while the other type did not succeed. Nonetheless, this project would have been continued if it were not for the financial crisis, which forced the company to become more focused in response to the 34 percent turnover loss.

Company Beta: This company engaged in three business model innovations, two of which became a success (case 1 and 2), while one attempt failed (case 3). Case 1 involved the application of existing, and the development of new, competences and technologies in a new market segment. Case 2, an acquisition, was much more risky for the company, both in terms of investment as well as time constraints, and involved the development and exploitation of new technology in a new market segment. In case 3, a failure, the company "pushed" a radically new product into the market in an attempt to exploit a new emerging technology, without any idea of how customers would respond. Cases 1 and 3 were implemented using the company's existing organization. As said, case 2 was an acquisition.

Case	Result	Key content	Organization
A	Successful	Existing and new technology for new market segment	New BU
B	Partly successful	Existing technology for new market segment	New BU
C	Failure	Existing technology for new market segment Outsourced M&S	New BU Partner
D	Successful	New technology for new market segment	Joint venture
E	Successful	(mostly) Existing technology for new market segment	Joint venture
F	Successful	New technology for new market segment	Joint venture: planned to be divested soon
G	Failure	Outsourced manufacturing	Supplier
1	Successful	Existing and new technology for new market segment	Existing core business, improved through BPR
2	Successful	New technology for new market segment	Acquisition; planned to be spun off soon
3	Failure	New technology for existing and new market segments	Existing core business

Table 5: Key characteristics of the ten business model innovations

7.2.2 Rationality in choice under uncertainty and complexity

Company Alpha: In most cases (except case F), there was never a search process for new business models. Rather, ideas were slowly developed along the way based on their existing core competences (e.g. technologies, know-how). The company simply considered it obvious that existing competences would give them relatively easy access to other industrial settings. These competences include the ability to:

1. Outsource existing products and processes to a new partner (case G).
2. Transfer existing technologies and processes to another industrial setting (cases B, C and E).
3. Develop, in-house or together with a partner, and then transfer, new technologies and processes (cases A, D and F).

The challenge, in cases D, E, F and G, was to find the right partner to work with. The search for a partner, rather than the search for an idea, seemed to be the main challenge in these cases. Furthermore, in all cases except E and F, the company preferred to generate the idea and test it first internally, starting with a low scale production process, and to consider growth in due course (e.g. through a joint venture, or a new business unit). This replication of previous business model innovation processes seems to be a winning formula for the company, and is expected to be followed relatively similarly in future business model innovations.

All new ideas have to pass through three strategically oriented gates before they are allowed to continue further to implementation. At the first gate, the idea is presented to the concept manager. The second gate involves a presentation of the so-called initial proposition to the top management. At the third gate, the top management decides whether or not to commit to the concept that has been worked out, and to the detailed business plan that was developed. With every approval, the budget available for developing the innovation increases until, after the third gate, all the funding needed to develop, produce and commercialize the innovation is available to the innovation team. Further downstream, the gates are managed by a cross functional team (idea factory, R&D, production, marketing and sales), which provides the innovation team with the flexibility to manage the stage-gate process from gate to gate as they see fit. At each gate, the team receives a checklist that must be completed before the next gate meeting.

Company Beta: As was the case with company Alpha, there was never a formal search process for new business models. Radically new ideas emerged over the course of time, either through existing technological capabilities (case 1, case 2), as a reaction to emerging competitors' technologies (case 3), and/or simply to reduce cost (case 1). Furthermore, the failure of case 3 made the management team even more aware of the need to better understand customer demands as a basis for selecting innovation ideas.

Company Beta, too, follows a stage gate model for moving new product and business concepts through a process roadmap and development process. For each innovation project there is a steering group, which is situated at the gates. This group includes representatives from the management team and the R&D group, and a product/project manager as well as supply chain staff (purchasing, distribution). The business intelligence unit, however, is not involved in that process. For that reason, according to one of the company managers, the discussions in the steering groups at the gates are concerned with performance errors in existing products, rather than searching for wholly new products/businesses that could better meet present, and potentially new, customer demands.

7.2.3 Cross analysis

Both companies try to reuse successful business model innovation processes (new idea generation and implementation processes). However, while company Alpha is keen on pushing ideas and technology into the market place, company Beta is more in favor of adopting a customer pull strategy. Furthermore, both companies try not to repeat failures made in the past. Consequently, the failed outsourcing attempts of company Alpha (cases C and G) has led the company to re-experiment with familiar, "pushed", business model innovation processes, while company Beta, based on the failure of case 3, has chosen to no longer push new ideas and technologies into the market place, without consulting their customers first.

These observations has led us to conclude that instead of learning to improve, both companies tend to "simply" repeat successful business model innovation processes and, equally, "simply" to drop unsuccessful approaches. This lack of experimentation with new business model processes, and the lack of learning from their failures may decrease the growth potential of both companies. Yet, this observation is also confirming our statement mentioned earlier, namely, that in most cases, managers' strategic preference typically involves "more of the same" innovations (or, in this case, "more of the same" innovation processes).

7.3   Discussion: Single vs. multi BM innovation

As the cases suggest, there are many possibilities for innovating the company business model. A company can, for example, strategically choose to innovate the core business fundamentally by transforming the entire business from "as-is" into a completely new one. Cases 1, for example, is an illustration of such innovation scenario.

Business model innovation can also come in the form of mergers or acquisitions (e.g. case 2). In such cases, business model innovation is considered to be a highly risky process, since the company partly, and sometimes even completely, abandons its original business and core processes, and develops a completely new business that encompasses new processes the company was not familiar with in its past.

An alternative process to innovate a business model would be to keep the core business fully operational ("as-is" followed by continuous improvements), and alongside it, to develop additional business models aimed at serving new markets and operating in other industries than those the company was familiar with. Company Alpha, for example, was particularly successful in launching such business model innovation initiatives, as illustrated in Figure 22.

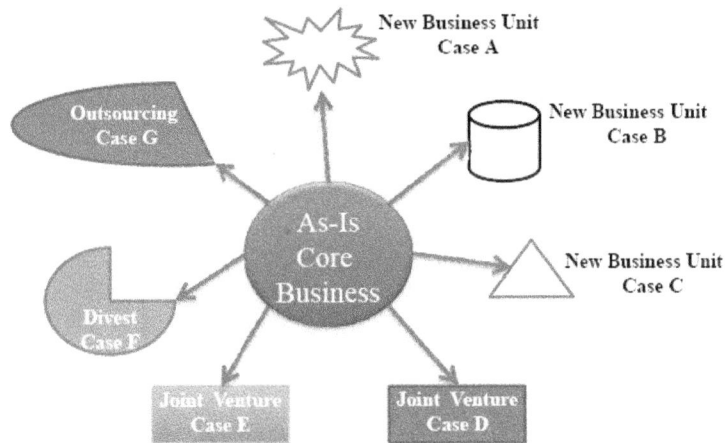

Figure 22: Company Alpha's business model innovation initiatives

On the whole, by embedding Chesbrough's (2007) open business model innovation thinking into our cases findings, we can argue that, on an aggregate scale, business model innovation possibilities can be perceived under three categories, namely:

1. Level of business model openness – i.e. innovating the "as-is" core business or (also) outside it.
2. Internal and/or external competences used through the innovation process.
3. Existing and/or new markets that the company is operating in.

Figure 23 illustrates what we argue to be the business model innovation "cube", where we have placed the business model innovation cases of companies Alpha and Beta in the accurate boxes for illustration (e.g. Case 1 – BM innovation that took place in the existing *core business*, using solely *internal competence*, aimed to serve a <u>*new*</u> *market*).

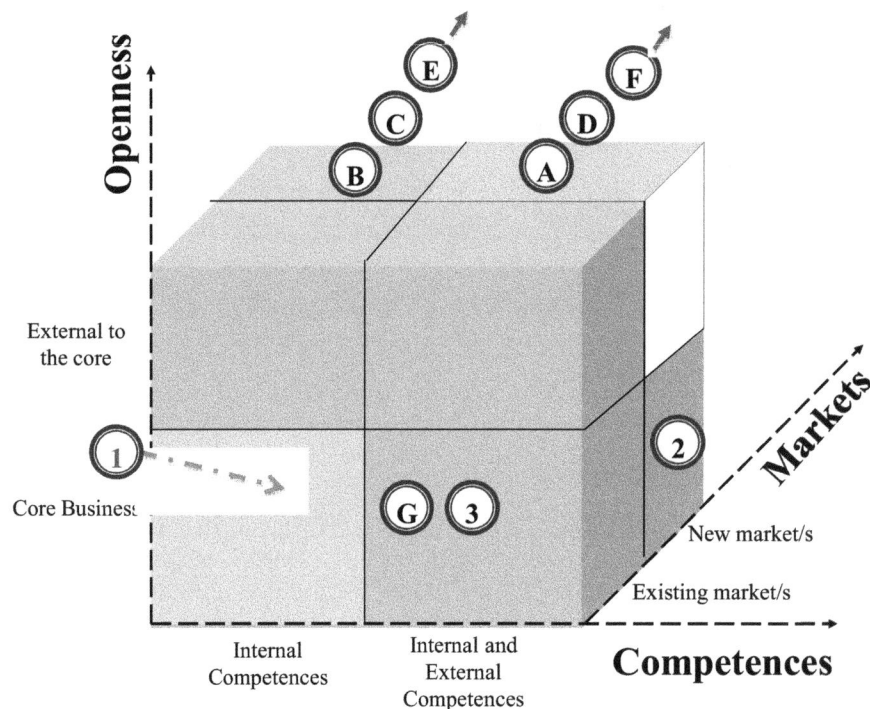

Figure 23: The business model innovation cube

As the model suggests, the BM innovation initiative on the bottom left box (i.e. core business, internal competences, existing market/s) will manifest itself as somewhat incremental BM innovation initiative. Alternatively, the upper right box (i.e. external to the core, internal and external competences, new market/s), will manifest itself as a multi business model initiative, and gives a more open view (Chesbrough, 2007) to the business model of the company. In these cases, a company choses to create a new business while still keeping the "as-is" core business fully operational – if the business model innovation initiative fails, the company could continue operating in existing markets, provided that the financial losses (due to the failure) were not too large.

Yet, it should be noted that given that all business model innovations are loaded with risks, it is still highly questionable which of the initiatives should be the preferred one to pursue. Open, network-based innovation also brings with it many (other) risks, and with that, new challenges. Obstacles associated with network-based innovation can manifest themselves as e.g. difficulties in finding a common value for the network partners to work with; in understanding the synergy (i.e. "who's doing what?"); in insuring trust between partners; in developing a joint profit formula; in securing sustainability to the new business; in securing intellectual property rights (e.g. Chesbrough 2007, Tidd and Bessant 2009, Miles *et al.* 2005, Dodgson *et al.* 2006, Ahmed and Shepherd 2010).

7.4   Conclusion

Companies today, in some industries more than others, invest more capital and resources just to stay competitive, develop more diverse solutions, and increasingly start to think more radically, when considering whether or not to innovate their business models. However, although many managers are very eager to consider more disruptive changes to their business model, they do not usually quite know how to articulate their existing or desired business model, or, even less so, understand the possibilities, or rather the processes, available for innovating it. The objective of this paper was therefore to propose several processes that are available for companies for innovating their business models.

The cases presented and analyzed here suggest that managers can perceive business model innovation possibilities under three levels of analysis, namely: degree of *business model openness*; (supply of) *competences* used through the innovation process; and *number of markets* that the company is operating in (Figure 23).

Finally, several approaches are possible to extend and test the results presented in this paper, including more case studies, to shed additional qualitative light on the findings presented here, or a survey, especially for generalization purposes.

Sum-up questions for chapter 7

- What is your understanding to the term "Business Model"?
- What does it mean to innovate the business model?
- What is the difference between product innovation and business model innovation?

8 Globalizing high-tech business models

8.1 Setting the scene

In the early process of the emergence of new international ventures, entrepreneurs are constantly in a 'tension extinguishing' mode as they are trying to ease tensions in the organizational gestalt which consists of mutually supportive organizational system elements combined with appropriate resources and behavioral patterns (Slevin and Covin, 1997). Two sources could be identified that effect these tensions, namely strategic experimentation (Nicholls-Nixon, Cooper, and Woo, 2000) and business model experimentation.

The strategic experimentation differs from the concept of strategic change in that it is not predicted on the assumption that these actions involve realignment of an existing strategy; rather, the emphasis is on forming and executing a strategy in an effort to reach a steady state for the first time. Entrepreneurs experiment with the business models of their international new ventures in an attempt to establish the dominant logic of the venture, whereby entrepreneurs reach an agreement on the way in which the business is conceptualized and critical resource allocations decisions are made (Prahalad and Bettis, 1986).

For example, tensions occur in decision making when entrepreneurs are required to determine the growth path of the venture. What shall the growth scope be: local, international, or both? What shall the international growth pace be: gradual or rapid? What shall the product mix be: only product-base, service-base, or hybrid product mix? How shall the venture enter the market: through dealings, structures, or both? What market entry modes to pursue? Will the venture grow organically or by attracting venture capital? Opting to attract venture capital, entrepreneurs are to deal with dyadic tensions that are the result of differences in entrepreneurs' and VCs' goals and measures of success (Turcan, 2008). Shall entrepreneurs look for strategic partnerships that may generate additional tensions as the new venture may become captive to the chosen strategic partner (Turcan, 2012)?

This chapter will focus on gestalt tensions during the early process of emergence of international new ventures. International new ventures are defined as ventures that aim to derive profits from international activities right from their inception or immediately after (Oviatt and McDougall, 2005). These ventures usually attract venture capital due to their potential for very high gains in combination with the availability of early exit strategies (www.nvca.org). At the policy level, international new ventures are seen as critical engines of economic growth (OECD, 2004). The data that are presented as part of the discussion throughout this chapter are derived from Turcan (2006); a summary of the data is provided in the Appendix.

8.2   Tensions at the inception

Since by definition international new ventures internationalize instantly at or immediately after their inception, the issue of whether to internationalize or not is irrelevant. The central issue then is how to internationalize. A set of tensions arise when entrepreneurs have to decide what business model to adopt. For example, should the venture be based on a product-led business model; service-led business model, or a hybrid business model in which both service and product business models co-exist? The experience suggests that in order to internationalize, entrepreneurs shall adopt product-led (or hybrid) rather than service-led business models. The underlying assumptions behind such decisions are the uncertainty and limited scope for growth, which entrepreneurs have to and eventually will have to live with in service-led ventures. Here is how entrepreneurs reflect for example on the uncertainty:

'We were a service based organization, like it or not. We were doing a lot of outsource development, which meant that you do not really build a sustainable value into your business. So when you start January first next year, you start from scratch; you do not have a number of contracts that are related to maintenance or whatever …it was very much a wish for us to look at annuity based revenue opportunities' – the marketing director of Finance-Software;

'I spent the late 80s going through a recession with my own business being in real, real troubles. And all you have to do is to go out and talk to people, and survive. That is the fundamental when you are a small, service business with no capital behind: everything is organic. You eat from what you earn. And that is it' – CEO of Tool-Software.

As to the scope, it is actually difficult to expand and internationalize a service-led business. Simply put by one of the co-founders of Finance-Software after an unsuccessful attempt to penetrate the German market: *'Services do not travel'.* The same view emerged from the discussion with an investor:

'Service-based businesses have difficulties to internationalize…just turn it another way: why would you go abroad in the first instance. I've seen IT-integrators who expanded to London: fair enough – London is a good, lucrative market. And, they started saying that they want to open an office in California. And you just think: why? Just because it is exciting and sexy to work in California! You have minor technology and your people are not that much down than them… They will do that for a year or two and after they realize how difficult it is, they will retrench' – the venture capitalist.

It is critical thus for the entrepreneurs to understand not only that service-led and product-led businesses require different business models, but also the fact that the transition from a service-led business model to a product-led business model produces tensions in the organizational gestalt: e.g., differences in the cost structures, levels of margins, marketing and sales, market positioning, and administration are the chief sources of these tensions as several entrepreneurs explain:

'At this point we felt that there was a need to establish more of a real company: to hire full-time development staff; to establish an office. …Selling services however is completely different pitch from selling the product. Services tended to be low volume, very high value contracts, over one year, or six months; but the product would be sold at a much lower price, therefore we had to be selling at a higher volume' – CEO of Project-Software;

'We always recognized that software is an area where if you can get the right software product then you can get serious amounts of money out of it. Because unlike manufacturing a product, there is no manufacturing costs; there is initial development cost, but once you have developed the product then the profit margin you get out of selling that price of software is very high' – CEO of Finance-Software.

These tensions that are built within the organizational gestalt have to be alleviated quickly by assembling and deploying appropriate resources in order to support the initial international development of the new venture. Entrepreneurs have at their disposal two generic growth paths to make this happen: either through organic growth or acquisition growth[2]. These paths are business model dependent. For example, entrepreneurs who aim to adopt the hybrid business model in order to develop the product might pursue this goal via organic growth. Entrepreneurs who aim to adopt product-led business model right after the inception of the new economic activity have a higher chance of attracting venture capital. Since both entrepreneurs and venture capitalists agree that services are difficult to internationalize, it follows that the growth path of a company is contingent on product-led business model and/or hybrid business model. Although, entrepreneurs' views on what business model to adopt may differ as presented below:

'As we were diversifying we felt that there were opportunities for cross selling between our consulting clients, i.e. to sell our product to those clients. At the same time we felt the need to keep those businesses separately, because they are quite different in nature' – CEO of Project-Software;

'Our move was very much to become a product focused business. The plan was to continue to make revenue from service, take some of our guys out of that kind of revenue earning, which was an investment in our part, and keep them, as an investment, working on the product' – CEO of Finance-Software;

'We started of as a service business. We had a working project in hand that we finished. That gave us some revenue to start with. Really the goal was to switch to product revenue. As soon as we developed the first version of the product, we focused on selling the product rather than the service' – CEO of Data-Software;

'We structured our business to product development. We also built a service capability, which generated cash and was meant to be project oriented at developing sort of tactical revenue really' – CEO Tool-Software.

---

2   Here, organic growth refers to the situation when entrepreneurs i) invest their own money to establish a new venture or ii) re-invest their profits to start a new business idea. Acquisition growth refers to the situation when entrepreneurs use external resources to finance these new economic activities via equity or debt.

The evidence suggests that international new ventures which adopt hybrid business models have a higher chance of surviving. Figure 24 below shows the strategic intent at the inception of new economic activities and the actual strategy at the time of crisis. Finance-Software, Project-Software and Tool-Software pursued the identified international business opportunities by adopting a hybrid business model, i.e. they continued providing services, and at the same time invested their own profits into the product development. Cases D and E, having raised initial venture capital, pursued the identified opportunities by focusing on a product-led business model. At the point of crisis, Finance-Software and Tool-Software were still pursuing hybrid business model strategy and were growing organically. Project-Software, having adopted a product-led business model, together with Data-Software and Mobile-Software could not cope with internal and external pressures and ceased trading. The following section will discuss the effects of these changes in the business models and the growth paths on the internationalization efforts of the new ventures.

a) Business models and growth paths at the inception of the new venture

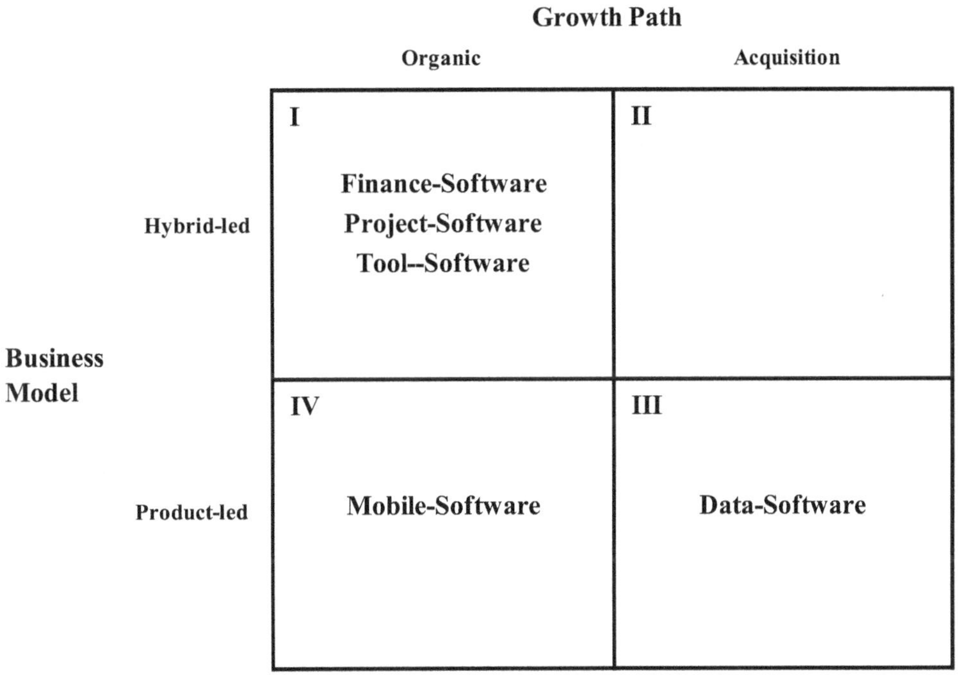

Growth Path

	Organic	Acquisition
Hybrid-led	**I** **Finance-Software** **Project-Software** **Tool--Software**	**II**
Product-led	**IV** **Mobile-Software**	**III** **Data-Software**

Business Model

b) Business models and growth paths at the moment of crisis

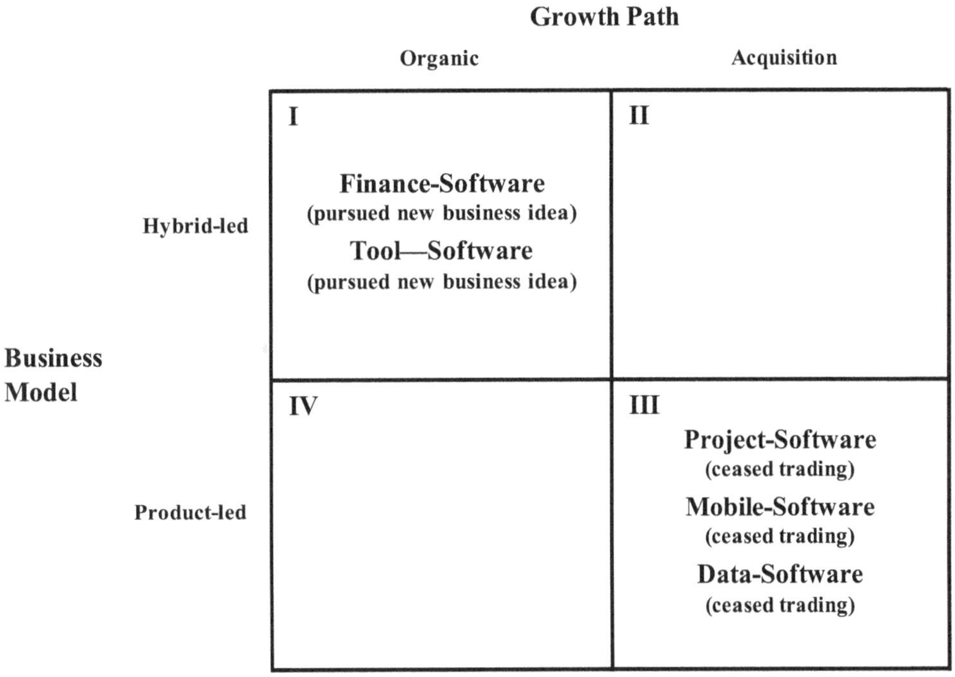

Growth Path

	Organic	Acquisition
Hybrid-led	**I** **Finance-Software** (pursued new business idea) **Tool—Software** (pursued new business idea)	**II**
Product-led	**IV**	**III** **Project-Software** (ceased trading) **Mobile-Software** (ceased trading) **Data-Software** (ceased trading)

Business Model

Figure 24. The evolution of strategic intent

8.3   Dyadic tensions

Entrepreneurs who aim to adopt the hybrid business model in order to develop the product might pursue this goal via organic growth. Entrepreneurs who aim to adopt product-led business model right after the inception of the new economic activity have a higher chance of attracting venture capital. These variables, however, might control each other in a loop. Entrepreneurs may change their original intentions of adopting a hybrid business model in order to pursue the product development under VCs' pressure and adopt product-led business model instead. Consequently, this vicious relationship may well be the source for disagreements and tensions between the entrepreneurs' and the VCs' agendas.

That is, as a result of receiving venture capital, entrepreneurs have to alleviate another type of tension: dyadic tensions. Specifically, these tensions materialize as the result of differences in the entrepreneurs' and the VCs' goals (Turcan, 2008). For example, entrepreneurs want to achieve profitability via long-term growth, whereas VCs' goals are to exit quickly via out-and-out growth – an agenda driven by the life cycle of VCs investment portfolio and the success rate of this portfolio as one VC explained:

> 'We have a target to invest from 15 to 20 million pounds a year. …The success rate on average is three out of ten are absolute stars: you give the business plan, and they completely deliver that. Then, we would see one or two out of ten would go bust; and the balance is somewhere in the middle' – venture capitalist.

As venture capital comes in, it pushes the growth forward, and it starts to climb the value curve. The ideal time for VCs to exit is when the internal rate of return that measures the investment retirement is at its highest value; usually within three or five years after the investment was made. It follows therefore that within a maximum of three to five years from an investment, VCs will look for an exit. According to one business strategy consultant, however, '…the strongest company is the one which forms the best relationships with its investors'.

Four types of goal alignment are identified: life changing opportunity; no marriage; illusive alignment and enslavement (Turcan, 2008). The ideal situation for VCs and entrepreneurs is when their agendas are aligned creating thus a life changing opportunity especially for entrepreneurs. As often expected, however, some entrepreneurs just do not want to sell their company. And if, as a result, no compromise is reached, then there will be no marriage between the two, as one VC explained:

> 'When companies are coming to us with a wrong model, we may question them, query them, they may change it. But if they have different view from ours, we probably will not invest' –venture capitalist.

These two types of goal alignment pose interesting questions for future research. For example, the importance of creating a *life changing opportunity* culture could be assessed by the value of the exit. That is, what would be the relationship between the alignment of entrepreneurs' objectives in terms of exit at the initial round of funding and the value of the exit? It might be conjectured that that higher value at exit would be achieved in those firms that had the entrepreneurs' objectives aligned in terms of exit right at the initial round of funding. Another pointer for research is to ask how different a value of an exit would be when the entrepreneurs' objectives converge gradually with VCs' objectives *during* their marriage?

When entrepreneurs and VCs do not arrive at a consensus and as a result there is no marriage between the two, researchers may delve into the effects of denials of funds. That is, what happens to the firms that were denied funding to pursue the identified new economic activities? Will they pursue other avenues for funding, give up and grow organically or fail? Crucial in this process of pursing other avenues for funding is the stigma associated with failure to secure first round of funding. The issue of stigma of failure becomes even more acute in countries like Denmark and Finland, where the VCs' community and the advisors' community are very small, and susceptible to collusion.

There are situations when entrepreneurs are ignorant as to the VCs' true agenda, hence the illusive alignment of goals. For example, when asked about the possible effect of VCs desire of quick exit on the performance of the company, the CEO of Data-Software was surprised to hear that VCs might even have this agenda:

'Do VCs want to exit quickly? I do not think that is true. We did not have any VC that was pressurizing for a short-term exit. They wanted us to grab the opportunity and maximize the value of the investment. Maybe some naïve entrepreneurs who are new comers to the game may believe in this' – the CEO of Data-Software.

In this situation of illusive alignment of goals, for VCs it is easier to mitigate the effect of getting an investment, which is when entrepreneurs lose control having actually retained the majority of the shares, via illusive control, by making entrepreneurs believe they are in control of the situation as long as they unknowingly and reflexively advocate VCs' agenda. As several experts noted:

'The day entrepreneurs get venture capital, they lose control, because VCs are using shareholders agreement/contract that goes outside share earnings to have rights to do things and to stop things firmly in the house. They have rights to positive and negative control, i.e. to do anything serious they have to do in spite of the board' –business strategy consultant;

'There is a side effect of taking VC money. In my experience VCs do want control. They want to exert control over the things that are not working. Typically VCs will invest in the business and the management team that is there. By and large they will leave it alone, if it works' – liquidator.

Entrepreneurs find themselves enslaved when they are trying to sell to the VCs their own business model and vision of growth, but VCs disagree and impose their own (Figure 24). For example, in order to get venture capital, the founders of Project-Software had to change their original business model and growth path from gradual internationalization (staring in UK, then moving to Europe, then to US) to rapid internationalization (going to US immediately, then to Europe, then maybe to UK). As the CEO of Project-Software explained:

'Our original pitch was to stay in the UK, get sufficient knowledge of the sales process, and then go to the US. At the very first meeting with our investors they said that this was a daft strategy; the vast majority of the IT sales is in the US, therefore you should be in the US straight away. Change your plan. So, we changed the plan, otherwise we would not get the investment' – the CEO of Project-Software.

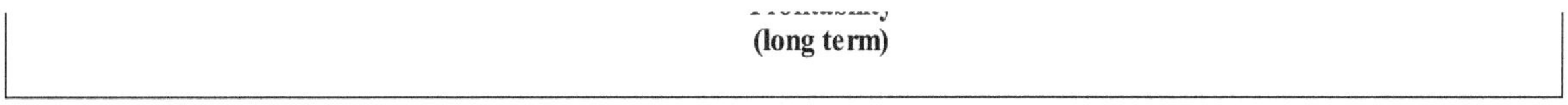

(long term)

Figure 25. Enslavement as the effect of dyadic tensions

8.4   Conclusion

As shown in previous sections, international new ventures go through several critical events in their efforts to internationalize, and constantly are in tensions extinguishing mode. Entrepreneurs are trying to ease the tensions in the organizational gestalt as a result of a change in the business model and growth path. To internationalize, international new ventures have to develop a product-led business model as services do not travel. Opting to attract venture capital, entrepreneurs are to deal with dyadic tensions that are the result of differences in entrepreneurs' and VCs' goals and measures of success. Dilemmas occur in decision making when entrepreneurs are required to determine the pace, the entry mode, and the international marketing mix of the international strategy of the venture.

Once through strategic experimentation and business model experimentation a dominant logic is achieved, the questions that most need to be addressed by entrepreneurs are: to what extent is the chosen organizational gestalt continuing to deliver returns and positive performance, and if less than optimal, what change would better effect attainment of projected targets. Agility plays a crucial role in effecting the desired and/or needed change. Agility is about flexible decision making and a flexible cost base structure that allow decision makers (entrepreneurs and VCs) to scale up and more importantly to scale down according to the activity level that the firm is experiencing (Turcan, 2008, p.295).

The other vital point in effecting a change is for decision makers to actually acknowledge that there is a need for change and act accordingly rather continue pursuing failing course of action. If decision makers eventually do recognize that the existing organizational gestalt is less than optimal, and decide to stop committing further organizational resources, the question then becomes at what point *too little is not too late* (see e.g., Turcan and Marinova, 2012).

Sum-up questions for chapter 8

- Which types of critical events do new international ventures go through?
- What is the difference between strategic experimentation and business model experimentation?
- Once through strategic experimentation and business model experimentation a dominant logic is achieved, the questions that most need to be addressed by entrepreneurs are: to what extent is the chosen organizational gestalt continuing to deliver returns and positive performance, and if less than optimal, what change would better effect attainment of projected targets?
- If decision makers eventually do recognize that the existing organizational gestalt is less than optimal, and decide to stop committing further organizational resources, the question then becomes at what point too little is not too late.
- What are the effects of dyadic tension on new ventures?
- Which role does agility play in effecting the desired change?

9. Communicating and reporting on the bunsiness model

The problem – as well as the prospect – with business models is that they are concerned with being different; as business in general thrives on some sort of unique selling point. So the bundle of indicators on value creation, business models, strategy, intellectual capital, and so on, which will be relevant to analyze or communicate about will differ from firm to firm.

Therefore, this chapter focuses on the business model as the integrating concept for reporting and analysis of strategic types of information on e.g. management strategies, critical success factors, risk factors and value drivers. Disclosure of information on these aspects, has in recent years gained importance, and several reports (Blair & Wallman 2001, Eustace 2001, Upton 2001, Zambon 2003, WBCSD 2003) and researchers (Lev 2000, 2001; Beattie & Pratt 2002) have argued that the demand for external communication of new types of value drivers is increasing as companies increasingly base their competitive strengths and thus the value of the company on know-how, patents, skilled employees and other intangibles.

Actually, the supply of information on the value creating processes and value drivers in companies is also increasing in various reporting media such as annual reports, IPO prospectuses (Bukh *et al.* 2005) and analyst reports. However, some firms, especially in the Nordic countries, have started developing Intellectual Capital (IC) reports that communicate how knowledge resources are managed in the firms within a strategic framework, and new models for reporting on stakeholder value creation and Corporate Social Responsibility (CSR) are emerging and gaining momentum even in finance circles.

Most literature on new reporting models and disclosure in general suggests that key value drivers that are strategically important should form the basis for the disclosure of information and therefore also the dialogue with the investment community, like e.g. financial analysts institutional investors, venture capitalists and news media. Traditionally, a major part of the fundamental analysis and financial analysis of a firm is a comparison with the performance of other firms and similar key ratios or non-financial information from firms in the so-called peer-group. This is, for example, typically used when financial ratios are computed and compared across firms, or when specific value drivers within an industry as when Revenue Passenger Miles, Available Seat Kilometres and Passenger Load factors are compared within the airlines industry or Combined-ratios are compared within the insurance industry.

Strategy, on the other hand, at least competitive strategy in Porter's sense, "is about being different", which means "deliberately choosing a different set of activities to deliver a unique mix of value" (Porter 1996). Thus, the bundle of indicators or value drivers that would be relevant for disclosure are likely to differ among firms, and they can be expected to be difficult for analysts and investors to interpret, unless they are inserted in the strategic context that determined their relevance.

A business model is concerned with the value proposition of the company, but it is not the value proposition alone as it in itself is supported by a number of parameters and characteristics. The question is here: how is the strategy and value proposition of the company balanced?? Conceptualizing the business model is therefore concerned with identifying this platform, while analyzing it is concerned with gaining an understanding of precisely which levers of control are apt to deliver the value proposition of the company. Finally, communicating the business model is concerned with identifying the most important performance measures, both absolute and relative measures, and relating them to the overall value creation story.

The point of departure for some suggestions in relation to voluntary reporting and management commentary is to illustrate the flows of value creation by linking indicators to strategy and supporting an understanding of them by providing a context giving narrative (Nielsen *et al.* 2009). Mouritsen & Larsen (2005) label this a process of "entangling" the indicators, arguing that individual pieces of information and measurements by themselves can be difficult to relate to any conception of value creation. As such, this "flow" approach is concerned with identifying which knowledge resources drive value creation instead of assigning a specific dollar value to those resources (Bukh 2002).

9.1 The demand and supply of value-creation information

The developments of the so-called Business Reporting models are closely connected with the need for greater amounts of information than companies are obliged by law to disclose in their financial statements. Furthermore, recent research shows a rising dissatisfaction with the current reporting and disclosure levels of companies. Sullivan & Sullivan has e.g. stated that the shift in the nature of value creation makes the valuing of knowledge-based companies difficult, because "[t]raditional accounting methods [...] are inadequate for valuing companies whose assets are largely intangible" (2000, 328). Furthermore, both academics, standard setters and professionals alike, express the need for more comprehensive business reporting. There are numerous reasons for this, including aspects such as better compliance between company management and capital market agents' disclosure perceptions, which can also be termed as a need for a greater focus on user needs, ultimately leading to more accurate valuation and thus a more efficient capital market.

In 2001, Robert Verrecchia conducted an extensive review of research in the disclosure field, dividing the existing research into the three groups: association-based, discretionary-based and efficiency-based disclosure literature. Despite the fact that Verrecchia's point of departure is the examination only of quantitative disclosure models, the field of business reporting with more qualitative oriented reporting models, can be associated with the area of discretionary-based disclosure, which Verrecchia describes in the terms: "The distinguishing feature of work in this category is that it treats disclosure as endogenous by considering managers' and/or incentives of firms to disclose information known to them; typically this is done in the context of a capital market setting in which the market is characterized as (simply) a single, representative consumer of disclosed information" (Verrecchia 2001, 99).

Business reporting being an expansion of the normal and regulated disclosures of the companies can be viewed as a public information channel. The need for additional reporting is seen as a result of the need for greater focus on user needs (AICPA 1994, Jonas & Young 1998). In the light of this, the focus on the development of reporting practices can be connected with the fact that investors are more interested in raw accounting data rather than processed data obtained through for example analysts (Barker 1998).

The results from Vivien Beattie's (1999) report, "Business reporting: The inevitable change", indicated already in 1999 an increasing attention towards non-financial information, even though this information still is weighed lower among analysts, investors and banks than traditional financial information. In general, companies, investors and analysts are becoming more aware of information about factors that are not reflected in the financial statements, although traditional financial information still is considered most important. In return, the respondents seem to be demanding more information about risk factors and reliable information about the management's qualities, expertise, experiences and integrity. This is evident in many recent Corporate Governance codes of conduct worldwide and in can be seen to some extent as a reaction to the financial crisis beginning in 2008. This kind of information is seen as a relevant and critical success factor for the ability of an organization to create value. This could be interpreted as a need for the type of information contained in intellectual capital statements and other new reporting models.

Various studies of investors and analysts' request for information indicate a substantial difference between the type of information found in the annual company reports and the type of information demanded by the capital market (Eccles *et al.* 2001; Eccles & Mavrinac 1995, Beattie & Pratt 2001). As the nature of value creation has changed from physical buildings and plants and equipment to patents, skilled employees and strategic relationships, directing more attention towards the relevance of disclosing information regarding the knowledge resources of a company. This information gap could therefore be due to an increased request for more non-financial information, i.e. company strategy and competencies, the ability to motivate staff, increase customer satisfaction etc.

There seems to be evidence suggesting that the stated information gap in effect finds its origins in a lack of understanding and proper communication between company management and the capital market and also that the capital market actually does value long-term strategic planning. This indicates that we might need to turn our focus on establishing a common understanding between company management and the capital market participants on the strategic intent of the company in order to solve this understanding gap. Maybe the answer to this lies in creating a common understanding of performance value drivers by reporting on the value creation process through a mutual business model understanding.

In the light of the tech-stock crash of 2000, it became evident that merely operating with a certain business model no longer is enough to please investors. Henceforth, profit generation was also required. Many efforts to support sufficient reporting on the value creation processes and business models of companies have been made. Examples of such business reporting models are: Value Reporting (Eccles *et al.* 2001), The Value Chain Scoreboard (Lev 2001), and the Intangibles Asset Monitor (Sveiby 1997).

In relation to the effect of non-accounting information on investment decisions, an experiment carried out by Catasus & Gröjer (2003) concludes that the possibility of creating reliable data about intangibles makes accounting for intangibles meaningful for credit decisions, and Solomon *et al.* (2000) illustrate that increased risk reporting is in the interest of the capital market, because it is helpful to portfolio investment decisions. Other studies conducted by Previts *et al.* (1994) and Galbraith & Merrill (2001) show that information on strategy and management experience is also incorporated into investment decisions, although it is important to take a critical stance towards non-accounting disclosure by questioning the reliability of voluntary information disclosed by managers.

From a likewise critical perspective, there are also signs pointing in the opposite direction, i.e. that the capital market is still not interested in non-accounting information. Johanson (2003) finds that capital market actors seem to be ambivalent towards information about certain indicators on intellectual capital, while other authors suggest that this may be because of the capital market agents' inability to understand how such factors affect value creation, including their own value creation chain (Holland & Johanson 2003), or that their inability to incorporate such types of soft information lies in the cultural aspects of the capital markets.

Still, the main opposing stance can be summarized in the words of Fenigstein (2003): "The value of any business stems from its ability to generate cash." It could very well be a problem that the capital market agents simply do not understand non-accounting information sufficiently. Garcia-Ayuso suggests that companies too are responsible for such a lack of comprehension and states that "managers must use a language that financial analysts and investors are able to understand. They have to provide explanations of the value creation process in the firm and make clear links between intangible investments and future value creation" (2003, 64).

9.2   The business model and business reporting

The point of departure for many of the recent developments in voluntary reporting, especially the so-called narrative models, is to illustrate the flows of value creation by linking indicators to strategy and supporting an understanding of them by providing a context giving narrative (Nielsen, Roslender & Bukh 2009). Mouritsen and Larsen (2005) label this a process of "entangling" the indicators, arguing that individual pieces of information and measurements by themselves can be difficult to relate to any conception of value creation. As such, this "flow" approach is concerned with identifying which knowledge resources drive value creation instead of assigning a specific dollar value to those resources.

Hägglund (2001) and Mouritsen *et al.* (2001) accentuate that the understanding of the value creation of the firm would be facilitated if companies disclosed their value drivers as an integral part of the strategy disclosure in the management review. Further, this communication would be even more effective if the framework for disclosure was based on a common understanding of the value drivers of the company (Bukh & Johanson 2003, Osterwalder 2004). Along these lines the business model may possibly enable the creation of a comprehensive and more correct set of non-financial value drivers of the company, thereby constituting a useful reference model for disclosure.

The problem with trying to visualize the company "business model" is that it very quickly becomes a generic organization diagram illustrating the process of transforming inputs to outputs in a chain-like fashion. The reader is thus more often than not left wondering where the focus is in the organization, and key differentiating aspects of the business model are drowned in attempts to illustrate the whole business. This is why the communicative aspects are so important.

From a narrative perspective, business models can be a support mechanism for projection of the management view to the organization through e.g. storytelling. The organizational narrative is also a kind of abbreviation supporting the ability of remote control, in essence constituting a representation of the business through a description; i.e. a story of how it works (Magretta 2002b) and the relationships in which it is engaged. A business model can therefore be thought of as a comprehensive description of the business system, including how the experiences of creating and delivering value may evolve along with the changing needs and preferences of customers. Such a narrative is an explanation of how the organization intends to implement its value proposition, much like the function of the knowledge narrative of an intellectual capital statement (see chapter 4).

The business model may potentially constitute a platform for the supplementary reporting of the company, for example, concerning strategy, value creation processes, knowledge resources etc. Generally seen, it is about communicating the company strategy, critical success factors, degree of risk, market conditions etc. in such a way that the investors realistically can assess how the company is actually doing and which expectations they may have to the future development. In practice, it has proven fairly difficult to do this in a way which is not too comprehensive and complicated, and which does not in an inappropriate way go too close to information which cannot be published, e.g. for the sake of legal requirements, partners or competitive conditions.

Internationally, several committees, commissions and groups of experts have during the past ten years worked on the development of guidelines and recommendations. For example, Blair & Wallman (2001, 59) have argued that the supplemental reporting from the company should reflect the dynamics which drive the value creation in the company. The communication and reporting from the company should ultimately constitute a representation of the company business model "by describing the relationships among the various input measures and outcome measures, and to link the primary inputs to intermediate inputs and, ultimately, to financial performance and other measures of total value creation" (Blair & Wallman 2001, 43).

In relation to the communication and Investor Relations work done in large publically traded companies, the business model may thus be perceived as a model which helps the company management to communicate and share their understanding of the business logic of the company with external stakeholders. This is often described as "equity story" in finance circles. These stakeholders do not only comprise analysts and investors, but also partners, the society and potential employees. This business model-bound equity story is related to the business-oriented tendencies within corporate branding. The main point here is that corporate branding is about rendering visible the interaction between the company strategy, internal company culture and image. Thus, corporate branding is an interconnected practice for the whole organization and not only an expression of the marketing department perspective. In this way, the notion branding becomes a question of explaining how the company earns money rather than an explanation of responsibility towards internal and external stakeholders.

The idea of equity story communication is thus that the uniqueness of the value creation in the company is taken as the starting point in relation to external parties. Sandberg (2002) formulates this in the following way: "Spell out how your business is different from all the others." Osterwalder & Pigneur (2003) consider the process which the management is going through in connection with a modelling of the company as an important tool to identify and understand central elements and relations in the business, for example value drivers and other causal relations.

Together with consistency, a firm structure for the communication of information and the very information may help the external stakeholders in the company to understand how new events affect its future prospects. In this way, the company can minimise the spread in the analysts' estimates which affect the uncertainty about the "real" price determination which, as discussed above, affects the capital costs.

9.3   Good advice on communicating business models

The problem with trying to visualize the company "business model" is that it very quickly becomes an illustration of the processes of transforming inputs to outputs in a value chain-like fashion. The reader is thus more often than not left wondering where the focus is in the organization, and key differentiating aspects of the business model are drowned in attempts to illustrate the whole business. This is why the communicative aspects of focusing the information are so important (Nielsen & Madsen 2009).

At the very core of the business model description should be the connections between the different elements into which we traditionally divide the management review. Companies often report a lot of information about e.g. customer relations, employee competencies, knowledge sharing, innovation and risks, but this information may seem unimportant if the company fails to show how the various elements of the value creation interrelate and which changes we should keep an eye on.

It is crucial for the readers' understanding of the business model that the company presents a coherent picture of the value creation in the company; e.g. by providing an insight into the interrelations that induce value creation in the company. Moreover, the non-financial reporting should follow up on the strategy plans and development in the business model in order to ensure consistency over time. As a business model should not necessarily be understood as a value chain, it should therefore not necessarily be reported as one.

A business model is also a forward-looking statement which goes beyond an identification of the immediate cash flows of the company. In capital market language, one would say: It is a statement on how the company will survive longer than till the end of the budget period. This means that when describing one´s business model, it is not enough to talk about the historic development of the company, not even if it includes an account of the company historic value creation, the company concept and how the objectives and strategy have turned out in the company.

Another central tool when describing company history is to support facts by non-financial performance measures. One thing is to state that one´s business model is based on mobilizing customer feedback in the innovation process, another thing is to explain by what means this will be done, and even more demanding is proving the effort by indicating: 1) how many resources the company devotes to this effort; 2) how active the company is in this matter, and whether it stays as focused on the matter as initially announced; and 3) whether the effort has had any effect, e.g. on customer satisfaction, innovation output etc. According to Bray (2010, 6) "relevant KPI's measure progress towards the desired strategic outcomes and the performance of the business model. They comprise a balance of financial and non-financial measures across the whole business model. Accordingly, business reporting integrates strategic, financial and non-financial information, is focused on future performance, delivered in real time, and is fit for purpose".

One of the keys to making management commentary matter to the investment community is therefore to emphasize the interconnection between parts of the narrative sections according to the logic of the business model. The next section looks at the differences in focus on the information types that relate to the business model between management commentary and fundamental analysis research.

We need to identify the most important performance measures that relate to the overall value creation story. We want to illustrate the flows of value creation by linking indicators to strategy and by providing a context-giving narrative. Mouritsen & Larsen (2005) call this a process of "entangling" the indicators [although we might call it interlinking and integrating], arguing that individual pieces of information and measurements by themselves can be difficult to relate to any conception of value creation. So we are concerned with identifying the knowledge resources that drive value creation – rather than assigning a monetary value to them.

Sum-up questions for chapter 9

- Discuss why the supply of strategic information might increase demand and vice versa
- What does it mean to entangle indicators?
- Give 3 pieces of good advice on communicating business models

10 The investor perspective on business models

Disclosure of information on strategies, business models, critical success factors, risk factors and value drivers in general has gained importance in recent years. Both policy makers and academics have argued that the demand for external communication of new types of value drivers is rising as companies increasingly base their competitive strengths and thus the value of the company on know-how, patents, skilled employees and other intangibles.

In parallel with the focus on disclosure of value drivers, the concept of business models has gained popularity. However, business models in terms of "ways of doing business" have always existed. The business model reflects the way of competing of the specific company, whether it concerns being unique or being the most cost-efficient company in the industry. The supply of information on the value creating processes and value drivers of firms has actually been increasing in various reporting media such as annual reports, IPO prospectuses and the reports of financial analysts. Furthermore, some firms, especially in the Nordic countries, have started developing Intellectual Capital (IC) reports that communicate how knowledge resources are managed in the firms within a strategic framework, and new models for reporting on stakeholder value creation and CSR are gradually emerging. Despite this, an explicit recognition of value creation as a central part of a business model is generally lacking in this literature.

It is also noticeable that even though disclosure of information from companies has been increasing, there are no clear signs that the particular information demands of investors and analysts have been met. The paradox is therefore that while there are well-developed arguments for disclosure and evidence indicates that companies are disclosing more and more information, there are also indications that disclosure quality is insufficient at the present. This leads us to consider whether we are facing a reporting gap, or rather an understanding gap. This is where the business model can be applied.

There is a multitude of evidence that the nature of the business environment is changing. Among the factors that drive this development are the globalization of markets, greater mobility of the workforce as well as monetary and physical goods and the application of information technology and technology in general. As the above factors and greater integration of capital markets cause changes in the nature of value creation, and new competitive elements gain importance, new types of disclosure and reporting that are argued to be so vital for conveying transparent pictures of the corporate well-being are unfortunately not without problems, as these types of information are somewhat more complex than traditional financial information.

It could very well be a problem that the capital market agents simply do not understand non-accounting information. Perhaps business models enable the creation of a comprehensive and more correct set of non-financial value drivers of the company and are therefore a useful reference model for disclosure. In the near future, western-society citizens will be questioning not just the future of the financial sector of the western world, but also the sustainability of the industrialized western society as a whole.

On the one hand, pressure from under-burdened western society taxpayers (voters) who crave an average working week of 35-37 hours and retirement 40-50 years prior to their death will be on the rise. On the other hand, eager hardworking Asian and Indian consumers with surprisingly well-educated workforces will lead us to be questioning our chances of economic survival in a truly globalized world all throughout 2012.

One possible answer to this problem is that western societies to a greater extent need to rely on human capital in the quest for private sector value creation, innovation and competitiveness. However, human capital will not make the difference alone. Only when complemented by triple-helix based innovation structures, creativity and unique business models that commercialize innovation and human capital will this be an avenue to future sustainability.

It is in this connection that the financial sector needs to start understanding new types of business models and hence also new types of information. Environmental, Social and Governance (ESG) information is a good example. It is today solely used by the buy- and sell-side in ex post audit society screening manner. We need to ambitiously pursue ex ante screening as a first step and then quickly move to actual active use of ESG information and information pertaining to sources of value creation in investment decisions. We should be hoping to see the first modules on analyzing business models and ESG information on post-graduate, MBA and CFA levels soon. At least for the sake of sustaining western society as we know it, we hope so!

10.1 Information needs of investors and analysts

While disclosure of information has been increasing, there are no clear signs that investors and analysts' demand for information has been met. Eccles *et al.* (2001, 189) conclude that managers "genuinely believe they try hard to give the market the information it wants. But most analysts and investors believe managers could try harder". Literature is abundant with well-developed arguments for better disclosure, and empirical studies document that improved disclosure is related to e.g. increased analyst interest in the firm, lower cost-of-capital and decreased bid-ask spreads.

Back in the 1990's various studies of investors and analysts' request for information indicated a substantial difference between the type of information found in company annual reports and the type of information demanded by the market, and more recent studies show only limited improvements with respect to disclosure practises in the firms.

Companies have clearly become aware of the importance of managing their external communication systematically, and the importance of investor relations is increasing. Also, investors and analysts are becoming more aware of the importance of factors not included in the financial statement, although traditional financial information is still considered to be of greatest importance. The general tendency emerging both from surveys of information needs and normative reports is that the capital market actors request more reliable information on e.g. managerial qualities, expertise, experience and integrity, customer relations and personnel competencies since these factors are considered important for the ability of the company to generate value.

Much of this information is, however, too complicated to summarise e.g. in annual reports. Furthermore, experiences from the management literature with respect to new strategic reporting models as for instance the balanced scorecard approach or intellectual capital reports show that it is just as complicated for management to define what factors are actually the few most important drivers of future performance, as it is for external stakeholders to understand such information when it is disclosed.

Related to this a recent report (KPMG 2003) based on answers from a sample of non-executive directors in the U.K indicated that while 94% of the respondents considered themselves to have considerable knowledge of financial performance measures, only 60% considered themselves sufficiently knowledgeable with regard to non-financial measures such as critical success factors, strategy etc.

Major questions regarding how this information should be defined, how it should be structured, and how it should be communicated to the market still remain to be answered? Furthermore, from the perspective of the capital market, similar questions arise:

- How should the information be used?
- How can it be trusted?
- How should it supplement traditional financial information?
- What overall framework can support the evaluation of the firm's strategy?

10.2 Background on the market for information

According to Ball (1996, 11), the theory of efficient markets is an imperfect and limited way of viewing capital markets as the prescriptive theories of finance on which the Efficient Markets Hypothesis is based, widely ignores the human nature of the participants that constitute the capital market and especially the three groups of opinion-formers:

- Company management
- Sell-side analysts
- The fund management function

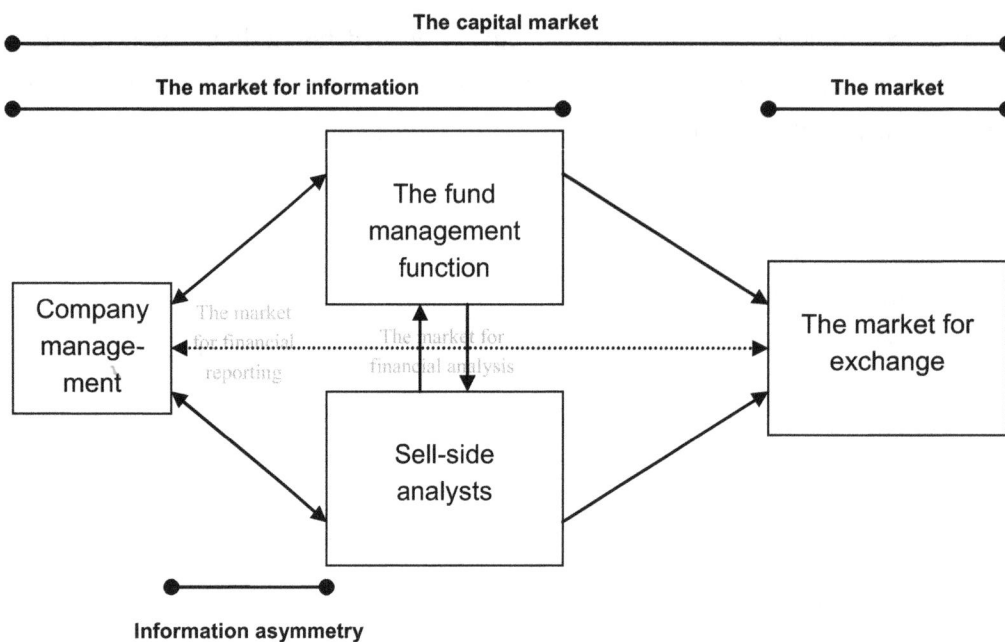

Figure 26: The market for information

In order to understand the functioning of the capital market correctly, we must make a distinction between the market for exchange and the market for information (see figure 26). This distinction was first introduced by Gonedes (1976), who argued that many of the assertions of traditional finance theory were misleading, because they did not deal with the relevant part of the capital market, i.e. the market for information. By relevant, Gonedes (1976) meant those groups of actors that were the major opinion-makers with respect to valuation, and he, furthermore, argued that "failure to explicitly consider the market for information may induce unwarranted inferences about the capital market" (1976, 628).

Barker (1997), depicting the relationships between companies, analysts and fund managers, argues that there are two 'information markets' co-existing in the market for information, namely the market for financial reporting and the market for financial analysis. In his subsequent study, Barker (1998) concludes that the market for financial reporting is of considerably greater importance than the market for financial analysis. With respect to the market for financial reporting, other disclosures from the company than merely the annual report must also be considered, e.g. press releases, earnings announcements and conference calls. The market for corporate disclosure might therefore be a better description. The market for financial analysis can be perceived almost as an intermediary function, however not neglecting that investors too receive information directly from the company itself.

Barker (1998) analyzes the economic incentives with respect to information flows between these actors, arguing that these incentives must in some manner also reflect the tasks carried out. Barker (1998, 16) finds similar economic incentives between management and fund managers, "both having a similar time horizon on a benchmark of relative share price performance, and both take great care to avoid negative surprises". Barker also concludes that because of the economic incentives connected with the turnover-based commission income of the analysts, the analysts in contrast favour share price volatility rather than stability (Barker 1998, 16). Despite the fact that fund managers consider financial reporting and formal meetings with company management more important than the analysts, their role in the market for information is seen as a "news agency and a source of valuation benchmarks" (Barker 1998, 16).

Holland & Johanson (2003) problematize the abilities of the market for information participants to incorporate new types of information on e.g. intellectual capital and the value creation process of companies into valuations. They argue that because the fund management and analyst functions have difficulties understanding even their own value creation process and intellectual capital, then how can they be expected to understand those of the companies they are analyzing and investing in (Holland & Johanson 2003)? Furthermore, Holland & Johanson (2003) argue that ambivalence towards using new types of information is attributable to the institutionalized nature and culture of these actors. This is accentuated by Ikäheimo (1996, 30), who argues that "[t]he value of a share is derived from a consensus based on the institutionalized conception of how the value of the company should be perceived".

The statements above bring relish to a dilemma and unexplored avenue in relation to the decision-making of the market for information participants. To minimize uncertainty and risks in investments, market for information participants and other actors in the capital market wish to base their decisions on full information, i.e. from a rational, consequential set. However, as indicated above, they do not understand new types of information otherwise regarded as highly value relevant. Therefore, although they want their decisions to look consequential, they are in fact characterized by the logic of appropriateness. Furthermore, as practices and rules-of-thumb to incorporate and understand new types of information are not presently institutionalized, the market for information participants face grave difficulties when packing and unpacking such disclosures.

Holland has conducted a number of studies in relation to the market for information participants and the dissemination of voluntary information between them. Holland (1998) concludes that private information disclosed to institutional shareholders is a significant part of a larger corporate decision concerning public versus private voluntary disclosure. Furthermore, Holland & Doran (1998) have examined financial institutions' application of private information channels, finding that these invested much time and effort in cultivating relationships in order to gain an information edge over the market.

In a later study, Holland (2002a) has found that the limitations of finance theory and the limitations of corporate disclosures and other public domain information sources cause uncertainty in stock selection and in asset allocation decisions for fund managers. Finally, Holland (2004) argues that the fundamental mosaic is the cornerstone of communication between the 'market for information's' participants. According to Holland (2004, 67), the fundamental mosaic: "provides a coherent means to tie together this information in a broader picture and to assess the impact on corporate valuations and it provides a means to check corporate promises against reality".

In 2009 John Holland refines his thoughts on the mosaic of information even further in his paper "Looking behind the veil": invisible corporate intangibles, stories, structure and the contextual information content of disclosure. Here he depicts three archetypes of value creation processes used for telling the business model story, namely 1) hierarchical (from top management), 2) horizontal (operational value creation), and 3) network (or alliances and strategic partnerships).

Holland explains: "The hierarchical aspect of the corporate value creation story concerned common structures and categories of strategic drivers across companies. The hierarchical narrative concerned the story of the board, its directors, and board committees as the primary internal corporate governance mechanisms. This narrative explained how the board chose top-management and incentives schemes, how top-management in turn developed and implemented a coherent strategy and how this was monitored by the board. ... The hierarchical narrative revealed top-down drivers of the value creation process. These primary drivers included top management qualities, coherence and credibility of strategy, management remuneration schemes, and corporate performance systems based on shareholder value."

Further, Holland writes that: "Each case company also articulated a concept or idea of its 'horizontal' or operational value creation process consisting of input sourcing decisions, transformation decisions and processes, and output decisions. This value creation process was normally conducted at middle management and employee operational levels. It was often the critical part of the corporate value creation story showing how a case company differentiated its economic transformation processes from those of its competitors in the same sector. ... The network value creation narrative sought to explain how the company sought to create many shared knowledge intensive competences at the boundary of the company. This normally involved the sharing both of tangible and intangible value drivers via supply, production and marketing alliances at various points in the corporate horizontal value creation process. It often involved sharing of unique or otherwise unobtainable intangibles."

Finally, Holland concludes that the business model narrative, or strategic story, normally connected many of the key elements in the value creation process. This was communicated externally to investors via a narrative connecting hierarchical, horizontal, and network value creation processes and the concept of an intangible, and its relative ranking, was given additional meaning by being placed and linked within the larger value creation story during the private question and answer sessions. This provided evidence and gave credibility to both the story and the relative ranking of the unobservable intangible factor. The combination of the narrative about the three value creation processes, the use of benchmark indicators or measures, their placing and linking within the story, all helped case companies provide the required 'full story' or 'big picture' to investors.

10.3 Gaining a competitive edge in the market for information

There is an intricate and rather delicate relationship between analysts, investors and management, which at the same time is located in an extremely competitive context (Fogarty & Rogers 2005). It is an environment of secrecy amongst the competing analysts, who all seek to gain some sort of competitive advantage in relation to their peers. The notion of having been or being able to gain a competitive edge over the market can mean a variety of things. For the financial analyst, there are basically three ways to do this; it can e.g. pertain to having information that others do not have access to, having a unique perspective, or simply to having better analytical skills.

Firstly, possessing a piece of information about a firm that none of the competitors have, is an obvious competitive advantage. As there are strict rules and regulations with respect to having price sensitive insider information, this sort of competitive edge is typically mobilized through expert contacts, e.g. specialists in the specific field of a specific company or through collaboration across offices within the larger investment banks. In this manner, having an information edge is more likely to mean having a more detailed account of existing information, rather than new information that nobody else has.

In this respect, having a good relationship with company management teams and investor relations departments is a key to gaining a competitive edge, as more details on specific elements of the firm (Barker 1998, 16) or e.g. an alternative management perspective on a piece of information might be shared through private dialogue. According to Francis & Philbrick (1993), the analyst relies on his relationships with corporate executives for information and analysis that is not widely disseminated. Such relationships, which may be conducted through visits to corporate headquarters, telephone calls with senior executives, or in group settings, are crucial to the analyst in establishing his claim to expertise (Philips & Zuckerman 2001, 393), i.e. competitive edge.

Also in relation to new information, the ability to be quicker to the market than competitors with newly disclosed information, e.g. in connection with earnings announcements, is another important competitive advantage. Typically, trading is stopped for 2 minutes around an earnings announcement. Within this interval the analyst must download and skim the report and be able to point out the direction in comparison to previous expectations to the sales-desk. For some analysts this is a crucial part of their job, while others do not see their value adding tasks in this situation. With respect to analyzing the company, having a competitive edge can either come through being the fastest, e.g. in connection with earnings announcements, or having the best analytical capabilities.

A key competitive edge, an analytical edge, is being the best at interpreting existing information. Frankel *et al.* (2002) find that analyst research helps prices reflect information about a security's fundamentals. This indicates that while the analysts' role may restrict itself to merely pre-announcing earnings numbers in connection with annual earnings announcements etc., their real value-adding activities relate to the more fundamental research and understanding of the company value creation logic, strategy etc.

Typically, the analysts create informativeness in comparison to the fund managers themselves and thus justify their existence by specializing by industry (Al-Debie & Walker 1999, 262) and by utilizing synergies between research functions within the investment bank. In relation to this, Desai, Liang & Singh (2000) find that stocks recommended by analysts following a single industry outperform those recommended by analysts following multiple industries. Hence, also the precision of their forecasts, which is a key point on which they are evaluated by investors, is a competitive edge.

Analysts seem to have their raison d´être where complexity is greatest. However, there is also evidence that even analysts have difficulties in making forecasts in certain situations, e.g. where knowledge-resources constitute a major part of the company value (Lee 2001), difficulties that could pertain to the inadequate applicability of conventional measurement and valuation approaches for such purposes (Lee 2001, Garcia-Ayuso 2003). Plumlee (2003) finds that information complexity imposes sufficient costs even on expert users and reduces their use hereof. Therefore, analysts' abilities to incorporate complex information in their analyses are a decreasing function of complexity and information processing costs. For instance, Bukh (2003, 53) argues that disclosing intellectual capital indicators without disclosing the business model that explains their interconnectedness leaves the analysts to do all the interpretation; something which they are not capable of. Garcia-Ayuso (2003, pp 60-61) questions the credibility of analyst recommendations in this light, vindicating for a bounded rationality perspective on analysts' cognitive abilities.

Investors and companies rank analysts differently, and even though some analysts are not the most accurate, they can still have the highest rating because their competitive edge comes from their ability to provide e.g. a new perspective on the firm (Beunza & Garud 2004, 14). Therefore, having a perspective edge, also termed 'a unique case', is a source of competitive edge. Beunza & Garud (2004) conceive analysts as makers of calculative frames. Analysts calculate, but they do so within a framework. According to Beunza & Garud (2004), analysts may appear to conform, but they also deviate from the pack to generate original perspectives on the value of a security, and, occasionally, displace prevailing frames.

The analysts rely on the factors mentioned above to gain an advantageous standing in the eyes of the investors, who then, in turn, trade through the analysts' investment banks and furthermore participate in rating the analysts among one another (Phillips & Zuckerman 2001). Typically, analyst ratings are a proxy for how much of their trading volume the investors will place at the respective investment banks, and as trading volume is what pays for the analyst services provided, the analysts live and die by their rating; hence the degree of competitiveness between analysts. Because analysts are dependent upon their customers, the investors, for their survival, it is appropriate to consider analyst reports as proxies for investors' information demands.

From the analyst point of view, indicators disclosed in the annual report or in a supplementary report only constitute one part, maybe even an inferior part, of the information needed to make recommendations to clients, because they are in a privileged position to "get more information – and sooner – than all except the very largest investors" (Eccles *et al.* 2001, 274) . It might be that the information has value relevance, but the analysts have already a much more detailed understanding about e.g. the research and development activities, than that which can be gained from reading about the aggregated research and development expenses.

Taking the above description of the different angles towards gaining competitive advantage as the point of departure, let us briefly reflect upon how different 'types' of analysts position themselves accordingly within the market for financial analysis. Analysts are not a homogenous group of people (cf. Day 1986), although it has been suggested that their behaviour and understanding of social norms are indeed extremely similar (cf. Norberg 2001, Holland & Johanson 2003). In the following, let us distinguish between two types of analysts, namely the small cluster and the large cluster analysts, where cluster refers to the amount of companies they actively follow on a daily basis. The large cluster analysts typically focus on 10-20 different companies, whereas the small cluster analysts concentrate on 4-8 companies.

There are large discrepancies between their job descriptions, i.e. their client contact activities, and also with respect to the customer segments that they serve, i.e. private or institutional investors. Generally, the large cluster analysts have more and smaller clients, while the small cluster analysts generally serve fewer and larger institutional clients. Also, the large cluster analysts have a closer connection with the traders of their respective investment banks – some of them even taking orders from clients.

These differences also have an effect on the type and detail of the research that they conduct and the thoroughness of the analyst reports in which they disseminate their results. Like with the analysts, there are also two types of analyst reports; the scheduled or earnings analyst report, and the fundamental analyst report, where fundamental analysis can be described as determining the value of corporate securities by a careful examination of key value drivers such as earnings, risk, growth and competitive position (Lev & Thiagarajan 1993, 190). Not all analysts conduct the so-called fundamental analyses, as it is not a part of their job descriptions. This typically relates to the type of analyst in question. This will be discussed further in connection with evidence provided in the empirical analysis below. As this paper focuses on gaining knowledge about how corporate reporting can be enhanced by investigating the types of information analysts consider important in their fundamental research, the point of departure for the empirical analysis will be fundamental analyst reports.

Studying financial data in relation to analysts' decision-making processes, Gniewosz (1990, 227) finds that the annual report is still considered the most important source of information (see also Brown 1997), although it is seen as having mainly a confirmatory function, rather than a primary information function, and a disciplinary effect on other corporate disclosure media (Christensen 2003). A number of studies have likewise examined the analysts' decision-making processes (cf. Schipper 1991) e.g. in connection with screening of prospective investments (Bouwman *et al.* 1987; Bouwman *et al.* 1995). A number of different foci have been uncovered, for example how analysts' decisions are products of group environments (Francis & Philbrick 1993), the identification of the most widely used valuation practices among analysts (Block 1999, 91; Plenborg 2002), and the uncovering of the various stages in the valuation process (Gniewosz 1990, Mouritsen *et al.* 2002a).

There seems to be some evidence pointing towards a context-specific use of valuation metrics. It has been indicated that fundamental strategic analysis is more appropriate for valuing younger firms but also more specifically new ventures, while the more capital-based valuation metrics, such as discounted cash-flow and Price/Earnings, are more aptly applied to mature firms.

Confirming the greater difficulties of valuating relatively new investment objects (the capital market's version of the company), be they companies, new ventures or spin-off projects, and also investment objects characterized by consisting to a great extent of intangible assets, Mouritsen *et al.* (2002a) depict a seven-stage model whereby the valuation process of such "businesses" can take place. In relation to this challenge, Hägglund (2001) describes more closely how investors and analysts work together in this process. Hägglund's research, focusing on the conceptualization of the company rather than its value, illustrates the complexity of the flow of funds to companies through the capital market and that the process also encompasses social and behavioural aspects.

Luehrman (1997) states that traditional valuation approaches may have become obsolete in the light of the recent changes in the nature of value creation from tangible to being predominately intangible of nature. However, the market for information participants still need relevant information in order to enable correct and accurate valuations of the firms, i.e. to get as close to intrinsic value as possible. On the basis of these facts, Mouritsen *et al.* (2001) suggest that three different types of capital must be valuated in order to get a correct picture of the value of the company. These are social capital, financial capital and "wise" capital, the latter including factors such as strategic knowledge and knowledge on organization and control.

10.4 Information trigger-points for investors

Events that cause significant movements in the stock price are called triggers. The term trigger is used in relation to initiating research and valuation of the company. Applying analyst terminology, trigger points are typically fundamental changes that alter the value of the company, e.g. changes to growth and value drivers or changes in the macroeconomic environment. In a sense, triggers represent possibilities for earnings surprises.

Possible triggers, points for stock price movement, and fundamental analysis could be (this is not necessarily an exhaustive list):

- The announcement of mergers & acquisitions
- Spin-off of existing operations into a new entity
- Entering into new geographical markets with existing product-base
- Introduction of new products to existing markets
- Significant cost-cutting initiations
- Change of strategic focus, e.g. from being low-cost producer to producing high quality products
- Changes in the top management team
- Announcement of passed stage gates in the R&D pipeline for future products
- Announcement of significant collaborative agreements in the value chain

Triggers such as those listed above do not represent information that can be put directly into an applied technical valuation model. Rather they represent key points in relation to the actors' fundamental mosaic. The perception of company value is determined by the realization of strategic options and future strategic choices made by company management. In this respect, e.g. quality of management, track record, strategic focus etc. become crucial for estimating the future performance of the company. The mosaic is a part of this understanding of how the fundamentals of the company will perform beyond the reach of certain cash flow estimates. Therefore, unpacking the black-box of the capital market actors' fundamental mosaic and its relationship to stock price is an important aspect to investigate.

The fundamental mosaic is the image of the company which each market for information participant has. Skubic & McGoun (2000, 17) suggest that communication of the corporate 'image', i.e. the fundamental mosaic, is necessary to attract attention to the company, i.e. increase analyst following (Wyatt & Wong 2002), enhance the credibility of disclosures, and facilitate the market for information participants' interpretation, because investment decisions are based on images rather than propositions. In essence, Skubic & McGoun (2000) here argue that a consequential understanding of the company is not what actually takes place. Rather, an appropriate representation of the company, like in the concept of business models is the basis for conceptualization and communication.

10.5 Analysts as infomediaries

The analysts, serving as information intermediaries between companies and investors, take multiple sources of information into account in their recommendations (Barron *et al.* 2002). This means that the analysts' reports, recommendations, and analyses are a separate 'secondary' source of information for the fund management function (Caramanolis-Cötelli *et al.* 1999; Holland & Johansen 2003, 467), and the analysts themselves act as sparring partners for the investors. Research confirms that investors react to e.g. financial analysts' research reports (Hirst, Koonce & Simko 1995), and also brokerage analysts' recommendations have investment value (Womack 1996), although Krishnan & Booker (2002) only find analyst recommendations to reduce investors' disposition errors in cases where they are supported by additional information in the form of a report.

There has been a lot of talk in recent years of the need to promote greater transparency in the communication from companies to the capital markets. Transparency is in the eyes of the beholder and is not equivalent to information availability or an objective condition to which organizations need to adapt. Therefore transparency is an outcome of internal and external stakeholders', i.e. company management and capital market agents, agreements on which information should be disclosed, i.e. a common conceptualization of the company business model.

Communication is often associated with information, the rationale being that a demand for more or better communication simply means more information. In the light of bounded rationality this becomes a problem, as external audiences have both limited access to information and limited information processing capacity. Equating communication to information is like presuming that messages are simply transferred from a sender to a receiver in accordance with the intentions of the former.

Communication between company management and analysts and investors can take place through a number of different information channels. Such disclosures can be conveyed through e.g. analyst meetings or open and closed conference calls. Private channels are found to be an important medium for disclosing supplementary information about the company. Research confirms that the financial report still is the most important information source to users of company reporting, regardless of their status as professional or private users.

Lee & Tweedie's twin studies (1977, 1981) examined first the private investors' and secondly the institutional investors' perceptions of the usefulness of the corporate report. They argue that even though there seems to be information symmetry between the investor groups, meaning that private investors get the same information as the large institutional investors, there is to a great extent an understanding asymmetry. They imply that financial statements are far too complex for ordinary investors to understand them (Lee & Tweedie 1977, 27).

10.6 Translated to the real world context this means…

In the above sections we have reviewed a lot of literature on the roles of the actors in the market for information and the information needs of these people. Below we will translate this into some pragmatic advice for students, young entrepreneurs and small companies wishing to enhance their communication with the financial sector in general.

It may seem as if there is a world of difference between the needs and desires of well-paid financial analysts and institutional investors in well-established capital markets with billion-USD turnovers and the young entrepreneur starting his own company, and looking for a few lousy bucks to sustain his ideas for another 6-12 months. Yes there is in some sense a world of difference, but the decision-makers are much the same, and their line of thinking is exactly the same.

For small-company investors (SC investors), whether they are business angels, pre-seed funders, seed capital providers, venture capitalists, private equity funds or other, investing is about taking a risk and being rewarded for this. Here information plays a key role, as information minimizes the perceived risk of making an investment. Transparency reduces uncertainty in the sense of providing a foundation for predicting future profits. However, information can of course create uncertainty, even if it is "good" information. For example if the information gives rise to several possible scenarios for the company.

Generally speaking, the role of the business model is in discussing and visualizing the ambitions of the company, e.g. is it a strong proposition, what are the scaling possibilities, can the company go global?

10.6.1 What does the small-company investor look for?

A SC-investor typically goes through an initial screening process of the companies that wish to engage in an investment partnership or sale. This initial screening process is sometimes quite rigorous, in other instances it is a question of assessing whether the SC-investor has knowledge of the proposed business area and competences to lift the business to another level, or whether they believe in the market the business is trying to address.

Surviving the initial screening typically means getting to present the company to the SC-investor board. Here one may typically expect a 30 minute session in front of the board where you should be talking for approximately 15-17 minutes and leave room for questions afterwards. In reality, the entrepreneur, or should we call him capital-seeker, needs to deliver his punch lines within the first 2 minutes. There exist numerous guides on which "business plan" information the entrepreneur should submit to SC-investors. The suggestion here is to construct 2 documents: 1) A report in a text format, and 2) A power-point presentation. Both could/should apply the following structure:

Front page	Including company name and contact information
Executive summary	A teaser summing the key points of the presentation • Which market is being addressed and how? • Market growth scenarios, quantified • Which user needs are being addressed? • What is the value of meeting these needs seen from the user? • How does your product/service meet these needs? • How much capital is needed? • When will we see a ROI? • What is the exit-plan?
The management team	• Who is involved and what are their competences? • What are the teams management skills? • What is the track record of this management team?

The Business model	• Which value creation proposition are we trying to sell to our customers and the users of our products?
	• Which connections are we trying to optimize through the value creation of the company?
	• Are there any critical connections between the different phases of value creation undertaken?
	• Describe the activities set in motion in order to develop the company
	• Enlighten these activities through relevant performance measures
	• Which resources, systems and competences must be attained in order to be able to mobilize our strategy?
	• What do we do in relation to ensuring access to and developing the necessary competences?
	• Can we measure the effects of our striving to become better, more innovative or more efficient, other than the bottom line?
Market analysis	• A precise description of the market
	• What is the size of the market?
	• Market growth scenarios, quantified
	• What drives this market and what is the elasticity on it?
	• Which customer segments exist and how are they addressed (differently)?
	• Documentation!
Competitor analysis	• Who are the key competitors?
	• Describe the competitors you are going head to head with
	• Do a SWOT analysis on these
	• In which way is the product/service of the company unique in comparison to major competitors?
	• What are the key competitors' product/market strategies?
Product description	• Describe the product so that its properties are understandable to anyone
Patents	• Are there any patents, patents pending or patenting possibilities?
	• What is the patenting strategy?
Go-to-market strategy	• Describe how the product will be launched to the market?
	• Which distribution channels will be used?
	• Are there any bottlenecks or initial investments?
	• Who are the key decision makers to address?
Risks	• Which risks can undermine the success of the chosen business model?
	• What can we do to control and minimize these?
Key economic ratios	• Forecast expected revenues and costs
	• Be explicit about the prerequisites for these forecasts
	• Indicate the sensitivities of these prerequisites
	• Give a base case, best case and worst case scenario

The investor role and exit-plan	• Which role do you expect the SC-investor to play in your company?
	• Which competences and network do you wish to gain access to from your SC-investor?
	• How do you see the SC-investor filling out this role?
	• Which ownership balance do you see?
	• When do you expect an exit and to which kind of investor?
	• What is your expected exit-price at this point in time?
Milestones	• Describe milestones that the company has already reached, like e.g. proof of concept, previous investments
	• Describe future milestones for the company and which impact they will have
Company description	• Provide a brief description of the company, including history, vision, mission and strategy
	• Domicile
	• Communication and organization
	• Describe key IT systems in place
	• Describe the management control system

Table 6: SC-investor screening

The structure outlined above follows most suggestions and guidelines in this field, but distinguishes itself by being more explicit about the business model. Ideally, the business model should play a larger and more central role in this process, but we do not feel that the SC-investor community is ready yet. They need time to understand the concept properly and therefore they still rely on a traditional business plan, sensitivity analysis and SWOT analysis structure.

10.6.2 The 60 second elevator-pitch

When you have prepared your investor pitch according to the structure in section 10.6.1, you should also work on delivering your "Elevator Pitch". The "Elevator Pitch" must be landed in under 60 seconds and it must answer the following six questions:

1. What is your product or service? Briefly describe what you sell. Do not go into excruciating details.
2. Who is your market? Briefly discuss to whom you are selling the product or services. What industry is it? How large of a market do they represent?
3. What is your revenue model? More simply, how do you expect to make money?
4. Who is behind the company? "Bet on the jockey, not the horse" is a familiar saying among Investors. Tell them a little about you and your team's background and achievements. If you have a strong advisory board, tell them who they are and what they have accomplished.

5. Who are your competitors? Don't have any? Think again. Briefly discuss who they are and what they have accomplished. Successful competition is an advantage-they are proof your business model and/or concept work.

6. What is your competitive advantage? Simply being in an industry with successful competitors is not enough. You need to effectively communicate how your company is different and why you have an advantage over the competitors. A better distribution channel? Key partners? Proprietary technology?

10.6.3 Looking out for global scalability

In reality, SC-investors are looking for companies that can position themselves for growth, because growth sells further up the investor-value chain. A recent comparative study on the Polish and Danish SC-investor community conducted under the auspices of the Center for Research Excellence in Business modelS, it is found that a further dimension to the framework in section 10.6.1 should be added, namely that of assessing the "Born global ability" of the company. Fejfer finds six aspects that must be considered in assessing the born global ability of a new venture:

1. Level of global orientation
2. Existence of global competitive edge(s)
3. Level of business model scalability
4. Managerial competences
5. Strong networking competences
6. Strong learning capabilities

Sum-up questions for chapter 10

- Discuss differences in information needs concerning business models between investors and analysts
- Explain how the various actors in the market for information are interested in business models and how this interest may differentiate between them
- How can business models relate to gaining a competitive edge in the market for information?
- Can changes in the business model be a trigger point?
- Which role can the business model potentially play for the analyst in his/her infomediary role?
- Discuss how the small-company investor can use the business model for his investment decision
- Make your own elevator-pitch for a company of your choice
- Why is global scalability so interesting for an investor and how can our knowledge of business models enhance the effect of this?

11 Analyzing business models

New types of disclosure and reporting are argued to be vital in order to convey a transparent picture of the true state of the company. However, they are unfortunately not without problems as these types of information are somewhat more complex than the information provided in the traditional financial statement. Plumlee (2003) finds for instance that such information imposes significant costs on even expert users such as analysts and fund managers and reduces their use of it. Analysts' ability to incorporate complex information in their analyses is a decreasing function of its complexity, because the costs of processing and analyzing it exceed the benefits indicating bounded rationality. Hutton (2002) concludes that the analyst community's inability to raise important questions on quality of management and the viability of its business model inevitably led to the Enron debacle.

There seems to be evidence of the fact that all types of corporate stakeholders from management to employees, owners, the media and politicians have grave difficulties in interpreting new forms of reporting.

One hypothesis could be that if managements' own understanding of value creation is disclosed to the other stakeholders in a form that corresponds to the stakeholders understanding, then disclosure and interpretation of key performance indicators will also be facilitated.

If firms report key performance indicators singularly i.e. out of context, or similar information without disclosing the business model that explains the interconnectedness of the indicators and why the bundle of indicators is relevant for understanding precisely the strategy for value creation in the specific firm, this interpretation must be done by the analysts. Currently, there exists limited insight into how this interpretation is conducted.

Hägglund (2001), studied the conceptualization of investment objects, and found that capital market agents' predictions of a company's operations are made in three steps.

1. They create a detailed description of the present situation
2. Short horizons are applied in order to reduce risk in the predictions
3. They construct scenarios that make it possible to categorize new events as they happen

It is a general conclusion that an understanding of the value creation in a firm would be better facilitated if companies disclosed their value drivers as an integral part of strategy disclosure. Further, this communication would be even more effective if the framework for disclosure was based on a common understanding of the value drivers in the company. Several authors suggest that business models can enable the creation of a comprehensive and more correct set of non-financial value drivers of the company, thereby constituting a useful reference model for disclosure.

From an accounting point of view, improved disclosure is more or less about determining the types of information that most significantly explains market value, in order that these numbers can be disclosed and fed into the decision making process, maybe even capitalized, but at least used for benchmarking purposes.

It is, however, questionable whether this would improve anything. The analysts and professional investors already have deep insight into a lot of details, and the most important information is likely to be related to the specific strategies of the firms and hence difficult to compare and interpret unless it is disclosed as an integral part of a framework that explains how value is created.

Since understanding value configurations and customer value creation is more of interest from a strategy point of view, a possible reconciliation of the reporting-understanding gap could for the firm be to disclose its business model, i.e. the story that explains how the enterprise works, who the customer is, what the customer values – and based on this – how the firm is supposed to make money. Exactly how this disclosure should be reported is not easy to say, but it is one of the issues that will be addressed in later phases of this research project.

In the section above, it is evident that a business model potentially consists of the interaction between many different parameters of the organization. Some unique business models thus involve extremely complex interdependencies, whereas, in other cases, it can be extremely simple to understand the specifics of a business model. An example of a company where a complex set of interdependencies create a unique business model is the Danish medico-technology company, Coloplast.

For Coloplast the platform for a long-term sustainable business rests on the interaction between the ability to integrate the ideas and requests of the decision-making nurse-groups into product development without renouncing the product quality perceptions of end-users. Measuring the performance and development of these interdependencies is extremely complex. An example of a business model easy to understand is that of Ryanair: "a ticket includes no service whatsoever. If you require any extras or have physical handicaps, then remember your credit card".

The notion put forth here is that if it is difficult for the company to conceptualize the business model, then it may be even more difficult for external parties to analyse and understand it. At present there exists basically no literature on the aspects of analyzing business models. However, several management and performance measurement models can be mobilized to some extent in the understanding of business model performance. Below, four perspectives of analysis are identified, each with differing ambitions and therefore also with different theoretical underpinnings, namely: processes, causality, quality and competences.

It is widely accepted that intellectual capital, strategy and other drivers of value creation constitute strategically important elements for the future profitability and survival of companies. Many firms already disclose much supplementary information in their management commentary regarding strategy, market competition, technological developments and products in the pipeline. Also, in the Nordic countries and more recently in a number of other European countries, companies have been experimenting with disclosing such voluntary and forward-looking disclosures through intellectual capital statements.

The problem – as well as the prospect – with strategy is that it is about being different. Hence, the bundle of indicators on strategy, intellectual capital etc. that will be relevant to disclose will differ among firms. For such information to make any sense at all, it should be communicated in the strategic context of the firm as this would show its relevance in relation to the value creation process in the company. In other words, it does not make sense to insert such information into a standardized accounting regime.

The SSA framework applies a risk-based perspective on value creation and combines the analysis of strategic and business related processes with risks and risk-controls to the identification of key performance indicators (KPI's). Thus, the process analysis template of the SSA framework helps the analyst to conceive how the underlying aspects of performance are related to each other via a risk-based approach.

The Balanced Scorecard's strategy map analysis is another methodology that helps to integrate KPI's and illustrates their interconnectedness. The Balanced Scorecard takes its point of departure in a cause-and-effect approach on competitive strategy. The strategy map methodology helps the analyst to link KPI's through the four perspectives of the Balanced Scorecard. The Business Excellence model is a quality-based perspective to identifying KPI's. Unlike the Balanced Scorecard, the Business Excellence model does not assume causal links, but rather a milder form of relatedness between measures.

In the section below, a fourth model for the analysis of performance measures is applied. It is a model developed for the analysis of the intellectual capital value proposition by Mouritsen *et al.* (2003). In its original presentation, the model was proposed to help create a set of rules for the analysis of intellectual capital statements that allowed the reader to appreciate the content of an intellectual statement in such a way that he or she could make an independent judgment of it. Later, it has been proven applicable to the analysis of many types of strategy-related disclosures, including voluntary CSR-reports, IPO prospectuses as well as the management review sections of traditional financial reports.

11.1 The analytical guideline

The idea of the analytical guideline was to develop analytical rules for voluntary information which paralleled the analytical concerns of the financial statement. According to Bukh *et al.* (2005) insight into financial assets could be translated to insight into the constellation of knowledge and value creation resources; insight about investments could be translated into insight about upgrading competences and resources; and finally, insight into performance could be translated into insight about the effects of knowledge, innovation and strategic choices.

The information 'input' for the analytical model can be derived from the information channels of the company which is to be analyzed; e.g. from the annual report, corporate website, management interviews or reports of financial analysts. In the case where an annual report is the supplier of information, the input thus becomes the specific indicators representing value creation, management challenges and the activities that the company performs.

The indicators are disentangled from the text of the annual report through the analytical model that organises the indicators according to three general problematisations of the firm (similar to the problematisations of the financial statement): What is the composition of value creation resources (what is the composition of assets)? What are the activities made to upgrade competences and resources (which investments are made in the firm)? What are the effects of knowledge, innovation and strategic choices (what is profitability)? These questions are concerned with the assessment of the firm's business model.

Evaluation criteria Knowledge resources	Effects What happens	Activities What is done	Resources What is created
Employees			
Customers			
Processes			
Technologies			

Figure 27: The analytical model (Mouritsen *et al.* 2003b)

Unlike an accounting system, the analysis model is *not* an input/output-model. There is no perception that any causal links between actions exist to develop employees and the effect in that area – e.g. increased employee satisfaction. The effect of such an action may appear as a customer effect: The employee becomes more qualified and capable of serving the customers better. The task of the analysis is thus to explain these 'many-to-many relations' in the model. The classification itself does not explain the relations, just as increased expenses for R&D alone do not lead to increased turnover in the financial accounting system.

From Bukh *et al.* (2005) the assessment criteria of the analysis model based on indicators attached to the three main questions of the analysis are illustrated:

Resource indicators concern the portfolio of the resources in the company, i.e. the stock and composition of the company resources within the areas of employees, customers, processes and technologies, and illustrate a starting point from which action can be taken. The indicators deal with relatively stable units such as e.g. 'a customer', 'an employee', 'a computer', 'a process' etc. They answer questions such as 'how many?' and 'which share?' and thus illustrate how big, how varied, how complex and how correlated the resources are. The managerial actions related to these resources are portfolio decisions; i.e. decisions on how many of the different types of knowledge resources the company wants.

Activity indicators describe the company activities to upgrade its resources; i.e. activities initiated to upgrade, strengthen or develop its resource portfolio. The indicators illustrate the direction in which the organization is working and help to answer the question 'What is being done?'; e.g. what does the company do to develop and improve its knowledge resources through e.g. continuing education, investments in processes, activities to educate or attract customers, presentations etc. The attached management actions are thus upgrading activities.

Effect indicators reflect the consequences or the total effects of the company development and use of resources. As with an accounting system, the model only shows the effects; it does not seek to explain from where they arise. The analyst may seek such explanations on the basis of the model, but not within the model itself. These indicators help us to establish whether we are arriving where we expected to.

Thus, when analyzing the interrelations of the business model it is possible to apply the ideas of a strategic narrative. Like all other stories, this narrative has a beginning, an action and an ending. So does the strategic narrative. It has resources, activities and effects. Together with an understanding of the company strategy and the key management challenges facing the executive management, it is possible to mobilize the questions of analysis illustrated above to identify the key indicators of the business model. Evaluating the business model can therefore be done in a series of steps.

A first step could be to evaluate the identified indicators in a scorecard-like fashion in relation to a set of expected targets for each indicator. Thereafter the indicators can be evaluated in the analysis model by asking which indicators affect each other. This analysis can be completed by asking whether some of the 12 boxes have missing indicators. Together with the indicators at hand, management should ask themselves how they fit into the story of what the company does and how it is unique. In this manner, management is gradually moving closer to its business model narrative supported by performance measures. In order to assess if the composition, structure and use of the company resources are appropriate, it is necessary to consider the development of the indicators over time, and finally the company may pursue relative and absolute measures for benchmarking across time and across competitors.

11.2 The process of evaluating business models

While evaluating the return on investment of a new machine, a new product line or entering a new market can be difficult enough, evaluating the potential return of investment in a new business model is even more complex. Problems of understanding, evaluating and valuing business models derive from:

- Lack of standardization, and thus comparability of the information
- Lack of time to analyze the information
- Lack of frames from which to analyze the information
- Lack of interest in these types of information
- Lack of correct form on which the information is conveyed

Plumlee (2003) finds that the complexity of information imposes sufficient costs even on expert users such as analysts and institutional investors, who, in turn, reduce their use of such information and this is of course problematic. The SC-investors do not really understand information concerning business models, as it is not something taught in finance at business schools around the world (yet), or, perhaps it is because they cannot be bothered learning it for themselves. Whether these provocative assumptions are correct or not, time will tell. At least we can conclude that business models are not a part of business school curriculum and definitely not a part of the existing institutions of the financial markets!

Transparency, here understood as the goal of communicating about your business model is not necessarily a question of disclosing everything possible. Rather it is about creating an appropriate representation of the company value creation. This raises two key questions:

1. What is appropriate?
2. But what is a representation?

The logic of appropriateness as a basis for making decisions can be elucidated by the following question: "What would a person like me do in a similar situation?" Rather than calculating outcomes, a person is motivated by appropriate behavior, considering which rules apply to a specific situation. Thus a person makes decisions based on his/her identity, values and experience which form a set of rules-of-thumb.

Below we will describe the most important aspects associated with a behavioral perspective on decision-making based on the logic of appropriateness. In general there are two different perspectives of financial theory, prescriptive and descriptive. Prescriptive theories are equivalent to the normative view of financial markets, encompassing theories such as the efficient markets hypothesis etc. Descriptive perspectives include the behavioral approaches to finance theory, also known as behavioral finance.

In essence, the disagreements between these two paradigms of financial theory relate to the inevitable discussion of whether human rationality exists *per se* or whether our cognitive abilities imply that bounded rationality must be the point of departure for such theories. This discussion leads to an account of two different perspectives on human action, namely human action as being based on 'logic of consequentiality' and human action as being based on 'logic of appropriateness'. The behavioral approach to decision-making is concerned with, "explaining how decisions are made in terms of motives, cognitive processes and mental representations" (Ranyard *et al.* 1997, 3).

Representation is essentially modeling, as it concerns creating images of reality. Thus images of the outside world are projected to us through representation (via e.g. some sort of 'technology', i.e. a business model or other management technology). Latour (1999) argues that representation becomes reality as it is a construction of objectivity. From his point of view, interaction is the essence of existence. Through interaction, objects become real only when they are able to be circulated.

Latour argues that 3D objects cannot be circulated, only 2D objects can (Latour 1999). In this case representation abbreviates complexity. Mouritsen & Dechow (2001, 358) emphasize this type of reasoning in relation to e.g. competitive advantages and competences, stating that these become 'facts' only if their mobilization is successful, mobilization being facilitated precisely through representation.

Cooper (1992) illustrates for us that representation is the transformation of the object – in our case the company – into a new form that produces controllability. Furthermore, influenced by Zuboff (1988), he argues for three underlying themes of representation; these constitute the mechanisms by which representation realizes this economy of mental and physical motion:

1. Remote control
2. Displacement
3. Abbreviation

Through remote control, symbols and other prosthetic devices substitute for direct involvement of the human body and its senses. Remote control thus underlines an economy of convenience by enabling control at a distance. The power of representation is the ability to control an event remotely, and can be described as a form of displacement in which representation is always a substitution for or re-presentation of the event, and never the event itself. The mobility of representation, created through displacement, is central to control (and thereby also to power).

Displacement emerges either as a transformation of the object, or as conceptual or material mobility, e.g. via projection. Displacement denotes mobile and non-localizable associations, while abbreviation makes possible the economy of convenience that underlies representation. Abbreviation, inducing a subset of the original object, is a principle of condensation, which enables ease and accuracy of perception and action. Through abbreviation, representations are made compact, versatile and permutable. Behind every act of representation lies the urge to minimize effort, i.e. the economy of convenience, also denoted as the principle of least effort (Zipf 1949).

When information is placed in the context of representation, it takes on a different meaning as representation is a more fundamental concept simply because information must first be represented in some way. MacKay (1969) supports this perspective in his definition of representation: "By representation is meant any structure (pattern, picture, and model) whether abstract or concrete, of which the features purport to symbolize or correspond in some sense with those of some other structure" (MacKay 1969, 161).

Information is that which contributes to the efficiency of a representation, thus providing advantage or gain. Representation and information are always preoccupied with the struggle for representational and informational gain (Cooper 1992) introducing the notion of decision makers, who change their representation of the problem in order to be able to reach a decision (Crozier & Ranyard 1997, 8). When perceiving business models as simplified versions of reality, representation becomes an abstraction of the business, identifying how that business makes money.

Let's say that SC-investors do not understand information on business models, which may otherwise be regarded as highly value relevant. Therefore, although they want their decisions to look consequential, they are in fact characterized by the logic of appropriateness. Consequentiality is therefore often sought in some sort of quantification or scoring process, where the business model is evaluated and compared to other "business models" on an aggregated level.

One way to improve these methodologies is to contextualize information on the business model in a series of performance evaluation stories. Here one might think of representation as a story, made up of:

1. A beginning
2. Action
3. An ending

All three elements must be present for the story to make sense. This business model narrative then becomes an abbreviation supporting the ability of remote control, in essence constituting a representation of the business through a description; i.e. a story of how it works (Magretta 2002b) and the relationships it is engaged in. A business model can therefore be thought of as a comprehensive description of the business system, including how the experiences of creating and delivering value may evolve along with the changing needs and preferences of customers. Such a narrative is an explanation of how the organization intends to implement its value proposition.

According to Holland (2009) the business model narrative, or strategic story, normally connected many of the key elements in the value creation process. This was communicated externally to investors via a narrative connecting hierarchical, horizontal, and network value creation processes. Holland writes that "Intangibles that were invisible to outside monitors were connected via the story to more visible intangibles and tangibles and to output and performance measures. Track record was then observed (made visible) by regular checks of the story against reality in the form of long-term corporate actions (increased R&D expenditure, new patents, innovation) and financial performance (earnings, EPS, cash flow, and actual growth in these), consistent with the value creation story.

The case companies argued that benchmarked intangibles set within the story were important sources of information. Some intangibles such as the effectiveness of R&D could be inferred from absolute (objective and visible) measures such as the absolute R&D spend, and by the number of observed innovations for this expenditure. These absolute numbers were ranked objectively, by case companies, analysts and FMs (fund managers), against competitors to get a comparative ranking. However, the contribution to value of many knowledge based competences or intangibles was difficult to measure. In these cases the key intangibles critical to a sector could be identified, and their effectiveness could be ranked on the basis of FMs or analysts subjective judgements, relative to competitors or the sector. Examples include the relative quality of top management, or the relative coherence of strategy. This relative, subjective benchmarking was the closest the case companies, analysts and FMs, came to formal or explicit 'measurement' of many knowledge intensive competences or intangibles.

This leads us to some practical implications for companies who wish to engage SC-investors (or other investor types for that matter) in discussing and understanding their business models. Firstly, focus on understanding the connections and the interrelations in the business. The core of a Business Model description is the connections that create value, e.g. between the boxes by which we normally structure the management discussion or the organization diagram. Remember that endless description of customer relations, employee competences, knowledge sharing, innovation and risks are more or less completely uninteresting to an investor. However, the really interesting point is how these different elements interrelate, and which changes and fluctuations that are important to keep an eye on.

How is the chosen Business Model performing can be assessed by analyzing the status on operations, strategy and the activities we initiated in order to have a unique value proposition are performing. Trustworthiness can be established through performance measures relating to the narrative. For instance, the business model narrative could be highlighted with non-financial performance measures.

Remember, that one thing is to state that the business model is based on applying customer feedback in the innovation process, but, it is something else, and more valuable to explain how this is done, i.e. which activities enable this, and what are the outcomes of these activities. Not to mention proving the success of the activities through a number of performance measures which:

1) Show how many resources the company is spending on the activity (illustrates the management focus),
2) Illustrate the level of activity and whether the company is keeping its promises, and
3) Show to which extent the activity has an effect, e.g. on customer satisfaction, R&D output etc.

Finally, this also enables the company to follow up on previous statements made by management and as such the business model narrative introduces a greater and broader sense of accountability to the organization. This accountability can be further enhanced by using time-series data on the identified performance measures. This would enable the company to depict a story of connections and relations and the investor/analyst to likewise depict his/her own story and discuss its implications with management. Below in figure 28, we use the analytical model to analyzing the business model story of a wind turbine manufacturer.

	Effects	Activities	Resources
Value proposition	Competitive wind energy	Lobbying activities	Brand and customer-base
Target customer	Percentage og TC and growth	Sales- and PR activities	
Customer relationship	Customer satisfaction	Developing digitalized CRM	Advanced key-account and online CRM
Value chain architecture	Smoothe construction	Project management	Logistics data
Core competences	R&D effects, new turbines etc.	Teaching use of CRM and digital platform	
Partner network	Higher partner loyalty	Hours spent on experiencesharing	
Financial aspects	Retain gross margins	Work with leasing institutions	Liquidity

Figure 28 illustrates how the implementation of a CRM system in the wind turbine company leads to greater customer satisfaction. It also visualizes a series of key measurement points that could be applied in an early-warning system on how this strategic effort is coming along.

Sum-up questions for chapter 11

- Why are analysts prone to not "getting" business models?
- Explain the differences between the three types of indicators
- Explain the steps by which the analytical guideline can be applied to analyzing a business model
- Explain how a business model becomes a representation
- Use the notion of a business model as story telling on an example of your own

12 Strategic innovation – the context of business models and business development

12.1 Introduction: a new competitive landscape

The concept of strategic innovation has risen to fame among management and academia – and it is still rising. And for plenty of good reasons too. The conditions for businesses worldwide are about to change for good.

Many different authors seem to agree that the external dynamics of industrial firms has increased over the last decade or so. Some speak of increased competition and the need for more market-focused organisations, whereas others discuss technological pressures on firms. Regarding the former idea, it seems to have become an accepted idea that whereas firms in the 1960s and prior could rely on stable (expanding) market conditions and customer-emphasis on price alone, today markets are less than stable and emphasis is on price, quality, delivery, innovation, and so on, (Womack et al, 1990), (Ansoff & McDonell, 1990). Ansoff writes: "...*From the mid-1950s accelerating and cumulating events began to change the boundaries, the structure, and the dynamics of the business environment. Firms were increasingly confronted with novel and unexpected challenges which were so far reaching that Peter Drucker called the new era an 'age of discontinuity'...*", (Ansoff & McDonell, 1990, p. 5). Hammer and Champy, in the 1993 book on BPR, writes of a crisis that will not go away: "...*In short, in place of the expanding mass markets of the 1950s, 1960s, and 1970s, companies today has customers...who know what they want, what they want to pay for, and how to get it on the terms they demand...*", (Hammer & Champy, 1993, p. 21). Furthermore, others place emphasis on the increased global competition from first Japanese firms, later Korean and other so-called Tiger economies, and their possible replacements in China and the old eastern Europe, (Quinn, 1992), (Kiernan, 1995).

In general, there seems to be agreement that an entirely new competitive situation has arisen. This is nicely summarised by D'Aveni under the concept of "hyper-competition", (D'Aveni, 1994). Hyper-competition, according to D'Aveni, is a competitive situation where the key competitive success factor is the ability to constantly develop new products, processes or services providing the customer with increased functionality and performance, (D'Aveni, 1994). In a hypercompetitive environment, firms cannot count on a sustainable competitive advantage, but must continuously develop itself in new directions.

Furthermore, there are also increased technological pressures to firms. It has become accepted that technological life cycles in some industries seem to be decreasing compared to earlier, (Foster, 1986), thereby putting pressure on firms to constantly innovate, (Kiernan, 1995). Much of this thinking stems from the electronics industry – for instance, the new generation of SEGA video games that your six-year-old plays with contains as much computing power as the Cray supercomputers of the mid-70s, (Kiernan, 1995). Even though this situation does not have to be equally dynamic in other industries – and, indeed, some questions have been raised concerning that issue, (Bayus, 1994) – it seems as if the belief in the technology dynamics creed is so strong that firms simply will follow that creed and, thereby, inflect the dynamics on themselves un-necessarily, (Nori, 1991). Either way, many authors agree on the need for firms to move technology up on the corporate agenda, (Clarke, 1985), and make it a strategic issue, (Bhalla, 1987), (Betz, 1989), (Jones, 1997), (Drejer, 1996). Further on the technological side, new technologies seem to arise that make entirely new ways of working and organising possible. For instance, Savage speaks of the possibility of "Fifth Generation Organisation", (Savage, 95), based on ideas of networking, virtuality, and so on. Using the same ideas, Martin discusses the notion of "cybercorp", (Martin, 1996), as an entirely new way of managing and organising firms.

The trends discussed above, of course, cannot be kept separate. New technologies have a strong competitive impact in general, (Tushman & Anderson, 1986), and hence the technological dynamics will also influence the competitive dynamics of firms. Bettis and Hitt writes on this issue that: "...*technology is rapidly altering the nature of competition in the late twentieth century...*", (Bettis & Hitt, 1995) and, in fact, guest-edit an issue of the Strategic Management Journal entirely devoted to discussing how technology will change the nature of competition and strategy in the years to come. Bettis & Hitt refers to the situation as "the new competitive landscape", (Bettis & Hitt, 1995), and it is this new competitive landscape that is creating a trend in management theory that creates the need for theory-building on the selection and evaluation of sub-suppliers, and the establishment of proper integrative measures to work with suppliers along a firm's value chain.

12.2 Strategic innovation: the background

Evidently, organisations need to be more innovative and think proactively in their strategic management. At least, this has rapidly become the mantra of the new decade both among managers and in academia. The well-known work on innovation management and technology management has gained newfound – or perhaps re-found – respectability and has begun to influence the way we think about strategic management as a discipline (Drejer, 2002).

On top of that a new set of publications have begun to emerge. These publications take their starting-point in the strategic realm rather than the innovation realm and, hence, focus on strategy and innovation or strategic innovation. A recent example of such a fashionable publication is Robert E. Johnston and J. Douglas Bate 's recent "The power of strategy and innovation" (Johnston & Bate, 2003).

This and other similar books – and the thinking behind strategic innovation as a concept – is based on three pillars (Drejer & Printz, 2004). First is the recognition by many that strategic managers need to consider both strategy for tomorrow and strategy for today in order to stay successful over time. This is now state-of-the-art knowledge within the field of strategic management – following the work of people such as Hamel & Prahalad (1994) and the 1996 acknowledgement by Michael E. Porter that strategy needs to consider both operational effectiveness and differentiation (Porter, 1996). Of course, Jim March told us about management as both exploitation and exploration in 1991, but let us not get into petty details about that. Secondly, the thinking is based on the well-known theory that innovation and effectiveness need to different kinds of organisation to succeed – from Burns & Stalker and onwards, we have come to accept this – and that this is because creative thinking per se is different from conventional analytical thinking as De Bono and many others have taught us. Finally, the thinking is based on the latest recognition that competition these days is less on product-markets or even on technology than on concepts and business models that change the rules of the competitive game, as, e.g., Gary Hamel observed at the threshold of the new millennium (Hamel, 1999).

In short, companies need to be able to manage their current set of businesses effectively while at the same time finding and developing new business ideas and models – this is defined as *Strategic Innovation*. Based on this foundation, Johnston & Bate (2003) assert that what is needed is a process to supplement the conventional strategic planning process – a supplement that they choose to call a Discovery process. The discovery process is creative and divergent and proceed the analytical and convergent strategic planning process in the understanding of the authors.

In short, we have a new concept that both encompass a desirable result to deal with the new competitive landscape – proactive repositioning of the organisation and development of new businesses – as well as the process by which the result is reached – a managerial process that is an alternative to the traditional, analytical process of strategic planning.

12.3 Defining strategic innovation

Early on Peter Drucker – and probably even someone before him – distinguished between doing the right things and doing things right (Drucker, 1958). When it comes to strategic management, we can reformulate this distinction to, on the one hand, market the right products/services on the right markets and, on the other hand, develop, produce, and distribute the products/services in the right way. It is intuitively clear that a company needs to focus on both issues in the long run while at the same time maintaining a dual focus on business development and operational effectiveness. The foundation for our work on strategic innovation, is that we think of strategy as:

- Change of the position of the company in the market place at the same time as exploiting the current position.
- The environment consists of both present and potential customers as well as a large number of different players, i.e. it is the entire environment of the company that needs to be taken into account in strategic management.
- The company itself should be seen as a holistic entity consisting of business and resources. This means that the strengths and weaknesses of the company should be described in the language of "bundles of resources" or competencies rather than departments or functional units.

In consequence, the potential of the existing resources to create value end different market places than the current one (while still creating value in the current situation!) becomes an important consideration in strategic management. One may speak of a competence readiness that the company possess and is able to apply by reorienting its business foundation towards new market places, i.e. strategic innovation.

As argued before, e.g. by Theodore Levitt in his seminal paper "Marketing Myopia" (Levitt, 1960), companies should define their business in a much broader sense than by simply looking at current products. Any business fulfils a number of needs and wants of its customers and can act strategically with much more than its current products. Hence, we may define a *business* as the combination of a business idea, a business concept, and a business system. An operational *business idea* is expressed in one or more products/services that are able to fulfil the needs and wants of a group of customers. The *business concept* is expressed in the value creation process – or competencies – that are the foundation for how the products/services are designed, developed, produced, distributed and marketed. The *business system* is expressed as the basic principles and procedures by which the persons and/or functions involved in value creation actually work.

This is a much broader perception of a business than the traditional SBU definition that is used in traditional portfolio management, mainly in the sense that a business here is able to respond strategically on its own.

We can now define strategic innovation as: "*Strategic innovation is the ability to create and revitalise the business idea and concept of the company by changing both the market of the company and the competencies and business system of the company. In this way, strategic innovation is concerned with developing the entire company*".

12.4 Defining business concepts

The idea of a business concept can be presented through Peter Drucker's (1993) "Theory of the business" model as a way of formulating the important issue of what kind of organization we have. This may be labelled a business concept and is a necessary starting-point for the strategic manager who wants to change his business concept.

Further, as argued before, e.g. by Theodore Levitt (1960) in his seminal paper "Marketing Myopia", companies should define their business in a much broader sense than by simply looking at current products. Any business fulfils a number of needs and wants of its customers and can act strategically with much more than its current products. This has been detailed further by such authors as Abell (1993, 1999), Markides (2000), and Drejer (2007), who have suggested a number of key concepts related to strategic innovation and business development. For instance, we find it important to distinguish between business concept and business model, which we shall see below.

12.4.1 What is a business concept?

Based on prior work (Drejer, 2005; Drejer & Printz, 2004), we can define the components of a business concept. As we saw in section 11.1.3 in this chapter, a business concept expresses the value creation processes, which are the foundation for how products/services are designed, developed, produced, distributed and marketed. The business concept is a somewhat super conceptualization, or meta-view, which permeate how inspiration is sought outside the current core organization and its businesses.

The purpose of strategic innovation is to develop new business concepts. Business concepts, in turn, may be formulated by answering a few basic questions:

1. Who? The first part of the business idea of a business concept is choosing who the business wants as its customers and, therefore, also who the major shareholders of the business are.

2. What? This is the second part of the business idea and involves answering what products and services the business will offer, and what customer demands and wishes the products are designed to cater for. Finally, the what part of a business idea will increasingly come to deal with determining how customers and other stakeholders are going to pay for the services/ products of the business.

3. How? This is the next basic question and involves formulating a business organisation, i.e. a choice of the competencies that the business is based on and a business model that determines the business' location in the value chain.

4. Why? Finally, there is the question of the strategic assumptions of the business. Is the business based mainly on a group of customers, on certain services or even on certain competencies and why? This determines a lot of things about the business besides the other issues of the business concept.

Note that what is outlined above is a much broader perception of a business than the traditional SBU definition that is used in traditional portfolio management, mainly in the sense that a business here is able to respond strategically on its own.

12.4.2 What are the characteristics of successful business concepts?

So far, we may summarize three things about a successful business concept.

First, a business concept implies a coherent and logical flow of answers to the basic questions of the concept that lead to a competitive strategic position for the organization in question. Second, involving customers directly is notoriously difficult in strategic innovation. Customers very rarely know what their present needs are, so how should they know what their future needs are? This is the very key argument behind concepts such as "lead users" and "user-oriented innovation", where customer needs are understood indirectly (often through anthropological methods) rather than analyzed by traditional means. It has been attempted to analyze what readers want from newspapers many times and the result is usually the same – we long for the kind of newspaper that we have always had, but we do not want to pay for it, perhaps because we do not have the time to actually read it? So perhaps what MetroXpress and other free newspapers offer us as readers is the chance to feel up to date in current affairs – even if we are not really so? Third, and finally, we may stress the importance of a unique and often groundbreaking business model in the success of new business concepts.

12.4.3 State of the art examples of modern business concepts

The next logical issue of strategic innovation or business development is to seek inspiration outside of the current business concept and organization. In order to inspire the reader on this issue, let is consider a few more examples of successful innovative business concepts and their corresponding business models, and mobile organizations.

The purpose of this exercise is, of course, to induce some knowledge from a number of new yet both well known and well researched business concepts and business models and may be compared to desk research as opposed to the detailed case study of the telecommunications industry which appears later in this paper.

12.4.4 Business concepts based on a new value proposition

In the newspaper and/or media industry, it is natural consider the Danish media company, Nordjyske Medier. Nordjyske Medier has sought genuine innovation in an industry where few others have dared to challenge the existing mental models. We have documented this case elsewhere in great detail (Drejer & Printz, 2004) and will summarize it quickly within this context. Nordjyske Medier has transformed itself from a local – and admittedly low quality – newspaper to a media corporation, with radio, telecommunications, the internet, a free newspaper a la MetroXpress (named "10Minutes", of course), as well as an old-fashioned newspaper. The key behind this transformation has been a rethinking of Nordjyske Medier's value proposition that led to the realization that customers are less interested in a newspaper as a product than in the information that is in the newspaper. So instead of seeing itself as a part of the newspaper industry, Nordjyske Medier has defined itself as part of an industry that brings stories to its customers.

In order to do that, Nordjyske Medier has had to redefine its business model and organization to have many more channels of distribution to its customers than just the newspaper. This has also implied developing new competencies in radio, television and internet distribution, as well as how to coordinate how stories are distributed across media channels. On the other hand, the basic competence of journalism has remained virtually unchanged by the transformation.

Nordjyske Medier has but one challenge. The corporation is still highly local and may lack economics of scale to create any real value in the business concept.

Example 1: Business concepts based on changing business in the value chain

Is it possible to do something similar to Nordjyske Medier but without the limitations of existing competencies and geography? By all means. Googlezon – the amalgamation of Google and Amazon in our opening scenario in this chapter – could combine Amazon's competencies in customer relationships via IT with Google's competencies in information search by offering customers exactly whatever content is wanted, when and where it is required. In order to achieve this end, it will be impossible to maintain the same location in the value chain as a traditional newspaper or even modern media corporation. Obviously, Googlezon cannot generate content enough to cover all the desires of everyone on the planet. It seems as if the more the emphasis on the customer, the higher the complexity of generating content for individual customers. For instance, Nordjyske Medier, which is among the smallest players in the Danish newspaper industry, still has to have a staff of journalists etc. in order to generate enough content. One can only imagine the kind of organization needed for a truly global media corporation catering for the needs of everyone…

Instead of attempting that, Googlezon will relocate in the value chain compared to media corporations today. The key to doing that is to let others generate content and focus on serving customers only. In order to do that, once again, the value proposition of the business concept needs to be redefined. How will Googlezon make money and distribute income down into the value chain? Will we pay per click? Per time spent on Googlezon's website? How does Googlezon pay for access from telecommunications companies and others providing the infrastructure? And how is content being paid for? Not to mention the largest stumbling block – money from advertisements, the big source of income in media today.

In other words, it is not trivial to change position in the value chain. It becomes necessary to define new organizational roles for the players in the value chain and make sure that everyone gets their fair share of income. Also the overall economy of the value chain may change dramatically. Consider what Dell did when reconfiguring the value chain of computers by "cutting out the middle man" and pioneering their direct selling model. All of a sudden the overall economy of the value chain changed.

Example 2: Business concept based on lead users implementing new technology

Getting new technology into the market place is notoriously difficult. Often technology push fails to deliver on its promise, whereas market pull is too slow and inefficient. But there is hope if one focuses on the right kind of customers. One way is to focus on the lead users that will pull the rest of the market along (Moore, 1999). The recent example of Skype show how extremely profitable such an approach may be. Skype was sold to Ebay for an estimated €4 billion in 2006 making it an interesting case of a successful business concept.

And what did the people behind Skype do? They did not, for one thing, invent new technology. IP technology had been around for some time and achieved little success, which was probably due to its low quality of telephone transmissions compared to conventional technology. So how did Skype commercialized the technology successfully? The answer is that the Skype people identified the right group of lead users for whom an internet-based telephone service was cheap and extremely welcome. This group of customers is business travellers on long distance flights. Skype jumped on the bandwagon, when airlines started to offer Internet access on transcontinental flights and so offered its services on the same flights. The quality was low here, but remember that the alternative for the business traveller was no phone calls for many hours (and being forced to watch the latest blockbuster film instead of working). So who cared that quality was low, the alternative was nil communication.

So business travellers jumped at the opportunity to answer e-mails and use a phone, i.e. work, while travelling. Furthermore, at the end of the journey they took the idea with them to their hotel (hotels are also offering cheap internet access these days) and the market has started to evolve. Upon returning home, the business travellers told their friends, fellow travellers and even started implementing the new service in their organizations worldwide. A worldwide success had started to evolve on its own – all because Skype had identified the right lead users.

It was, however, probably a good thing for Skype that Ebay came along with some money, as the continuous implementation of IP services will require an enormous amount of resources in order to succeed. So, €4 billion was probably a very nice way of unloading Skype to the next part of the "food-chain".

Example 3: Business concept based on Blue Oceans

These days we also find a number of business concepts based on the notion of "blue oceans" (Kim & Mauborgne, 2005), so let us offer an example of this interesting way of thinking. Car rental is a big business and one would think that the biggest names in car rentals – Hertz, Avis, Budget and the likes – would be making the biggest money. Not so. These companies compete for the same customers in similar ways, i.e. price, in a so-called "red ocean" (Kim & Mauborgne, 2007). Think about it. We only see these names in airports, admittedly all over the world, but still limited. The car rental company that makes the most money is not found among the well-known names and sizable organisations mentioned. It is a major surprise. Even though it is not (yet) Rent a Wreck, we are getting there. It is Enterprise from the US. And what have they done? We think that the founders of Enterprise might well have looked at the industry and its big players and asked themselves the question – do we want to be in the line of car rental companies in airports? And probably answered – NO! If we do that, we can only compete on equal or lower prices than the big names.

Should we manage to do that we would still have to accept higher costs due to lack of scale or, worse, from having to lure employees from the competition to join us if demand rises. In other words, we will enter competition in a red ocean with the inherent disadvantages of lower prices and higher costs than the competition – and who wants to do that.

So, maybe the founders of Enterprise went looking for something completely different, a blue ocean. Maybe they found this by looking at the customers of rented cars. Sure many customers, perhaps even the greatest proportion, are travellers to be found in airports. But what about the customers who are not travelling but are at home? Enterprise is based on these customers. This customer segment is located in the big US cities and they have a number of needs for car rental, where price is not terribly important. When your car breaks down and has to be replaced, you need an in-between car in order to go to work and so on. The cost might be covered by the insurance company or is just not very important. And so on. Enterprise has managed to identity a number of customer needs and requirements from a customer segment that no-one was interested in and based its business concept on these customers. As for a business model, this is also quite different from the models of the competition. Enterprise needs to be located in the big cities, where office space – and often even wages – are lower than in airports, and needs to master a set of competencies slightly different from the competition.

This business model has yet to be copied by others, so for now Enterprise competes in a nice peaceful blue ocean. And should anyone try to copy the business concept, then they would fall into the same trap that Enterprise has avoided falling into – the Red Ocean of car rental, the one with cut-throat competition, higher costs, and lower prices.

Example 4: Business concepts based on value-added services

Let us revisit Apple as a case. Whether this example is, in fact, also an example of finding a 'blue ocean' may be debated. No matter what, it is an interesting example of a business concept and business model, based on the Apple iPod. Apple enters a market that has stabilized in a fierce red ocean competition on cheap and very similar products and managed to take control of the market with a much more expensive and functional product. Not to mention a user friendly and cool product, but these things, we will argue, are of less importance to the business concept than the idea of value-added services. Of course designers seem to take credit for the success of the iPod, as do engineering people, marketing people, and so on. Everyone loves a success. We believe that the success of the iPod is a combination of an intelligent business concept that manages to combine the creation of a blue ocean position in the market with the opportunities for continuous innovation (as a means to protect that position).

If we attempt to formulate the business concept in words, we may end up with something along the following lines.

1. Who? Users of MP3 sound, who are ready to let the iPod play an important role in their lives and, hence, are ready to pay a premium price for the core product itself as well as apply to the value added services of the iPod business concept.

2. What? The iPod is a well conceived, well designed, user friendly product with a large memory and a number of other features, but it is also iTunes (buying music in the proper format on the internet) and access to the large community of iPod users who exchange Podcasts, music, movies, ideas and trivia through the net.

3. How? This is a complicated matter because there are property rights involved. As such, a truly digital business model – and iPod is based on such a model – is usually relatively easy to conceive and very complicated to execute. It is obvious that Apple have had to acquire a lot of competencies in IPR in order to get to a point where they can actually sell music digitally. Furthermore, a number of competencies in marketing via the net have had to be developed.

4. Why? As always this is a complicated matter to answer from the outside. However, we believe that the iPod is based on a strategic core ideology that is very aggressive and aimed at expanding the value added services of iTunes from music to, say movies. This will enable Apple to make a lot of money out of value added services, which is very nice, but might also just enable Apple to, finally, place an Apple computer in every home to deal with music and movies.

12.4.4 What can we learn from the four examples above?

If we are to infer something from these examples, there are three main conclusions. First, the concepts are all based on an outside-in perspective. Customer needs have to be the starting-point of business concepts and strategy these days. Often it is the future needs and wants of customers that enable the formulation of innovative business concepts. It is one of the main developments of modern strategy thinking that we have managed to get the customer as the starting point for strategic management again. Second, at the same time, however, it is crucial to rethink the aspect of the business model in contemporary business concepts. As much as we argue that the customer should be important to strategy, it seems clear from the examples above that contemporary business concepts are to some extent all deeply dependent on new competencies, new organizational forms and new ways of thinking about the business model of the organization. Finally, the success of new business models is closely linked to the design and implementation of mobile organizations and new forms of collaboration across traditional geographical, organizational, and technological boundaries.

12.5 Discussions

Now, finally, what may these discussions enable us to say about strategic innovation and strategic management?

12.5.1 Strategy theory has lost its way

We will assert that a large proportion of the recent and fashionable work claiming to be *strategic* in fact represent tactical areas and means to secure operational effectiveness – rather than the differentiating and innovative business development that we have identified the need for. Consider the contributions on Business Process Reengineering, Business Excellence, Balanced Scorecard, quality strategy, strategic technology planning, and many others. Even according to what Michael Porter relatively recently has written on "what a strategy is", these are contributions that are means to create operational effectiveness. Therefore, we must consider them tactical and precisely not strategic!

Based on this statement, we will argue that strategy theory has gotten lost after the seminal work on strategy as the development of products on appropriate markets (e.g. Ansoff, 1965; Levitt, 1960) combined with consideration of the internal strengths and weaknesses of the company (Andrews, 1960; Penrose, 1957). We feel that there is a need to take a step back and reconsider what strategy is about compared to what strategy is sometimes said to be about in its more modern manifestations. We find it particular useful to take a closer look at some of the seminal contributions compared to some recent ones and investigate if there is anything that justifies the differences. Consider a classical definition of strategy from Ackoff (1979):

- Strategic thinking represents innovative thinking about new activities and relationships at the organisational level. The key activity here should be business development understood as the development of products and competencies at the same time. The purpose of the change of the strategic foundation of the company and the unit of analysis is at the level of competencies and product-markets.
- Strategic planning represents the analysis and formulation of action plans. The key activity here should be the translation of business ideas and scenarios to consequences for the market, resources, structure, etc. of the company in order to find the opportunities for developing the company fast and correctly to the realization of the strategic thoughts.
- Operations mean the operation of the existing activities within the boundaries defined by the current environment, strategy and resources available. The key activity is small improvements, the unit of analysis is organizational units and the purpose is productivity.

Evidently, strategic management should be closely linked to (productive) operations, but managerially the two represent quite different tasks. Furthermore, we find that there are a number of research challenges related to the strategic managerial task that are unique compared to the challenges of the operations task.

12.5.2 Managers may not have…

It would be all to easy to make the assertion that top management teams in general are not "creative enough" and do not "think out of the box" when writing about strategic innovation. It is probably true, but often leads to the misconception that strategic top managers should only be concerned with creative thinking and innovation. Not so. Even the literature on strategic innovation is careful to propose a creative, business creation process as a supplement to the traditional (business administrating) process of strategic planning. And now, we can be even more specific. By applying a learning perspective, we can say that the top management group should be good at single loop learning, double loop learning and deutero learning in order to solve its task of strategic planning and strategic innovation.

Having said that it would be natural to assume to many top management groups are less skilled at double loop learning and deutero learning than at singled loop learning. The latter we would relate to strategic planning and budgeting, whereas the former we would relate to strategic innovation (double loop learning) and the balancing of strategic planning and strategic innovation (deutero learning). So how does a management team improve its skills at double loop learning and deutero learning? The two will be connected, of course. Double loop learning may be improved by applying new cognitive schemes in order to see the consequences of strategic action a new and breaking old mental models in order to think up new plans for future actions. This will then render it necessary to interpret knowledge and experience in new ways and create a whole new set of barriers to organisational change that should be dealt with subsequently, but the key to double loop learning – we believe – is elsewhere. As for deutero learning, this is improved by making explicit the mental models, cognitive schemes, experiences and knowledge and barriers to change and deciding when to adhere to them and when to break away from them. As such this is the very balancing between strategic planning and strategic innovation – or single loop learning and double loop learning – that we have defined deutero learning as in this context. And it should be noted that a making the thresholds of the team learning process explicit will, per se, make double loop learning easier.